Tell Me About
THE
CREATION

HARUN YAHYA

Goodwordkidz
The Children's Group of Goodword Publishing House

ABOUT THE AUTHOR

The author, who writes under the pen-name HARUN YAHYA, was born in Ankara in 1956. Having completed his primary and secondary education in Ankara, he then studied arts at Istanbul's Mimar Sinan University and philosophy at Istanbul University. Since the 1980s, the author has published many books on political, faith-related and scientific issues. Harun Yahya is well-known as an author who has written very important works disclosing the imposture of evolutionists, the invalidity of their claims and the dark liaisons between Darwinism and bloody ideologies.

His pen-name is made up of the names "Harun" (Aaron) and "Yahya" (John), in memory of the two esteemed prophets who fought against lack of faith. The Prophet's seal on the cover of the author's books has a symbolic meaning linked to their contents. This seal represents the Qur'an as the last book by God and the last word of Him and our Prophet, the last of all the prophets. Under the guidance of the Qur'an and Sunnah, the author makes it his main goal to disprove each one of the fundamental tenets of godless ideologies and to have the "last word", so as to completely silence the objections raised against religion. The seal of the Prophet, who attained ultimate wisdom and moral perfection, is used as a sign of his intention of saying this last word.

All these works by the author centre around one goal: to convey the message of the Qur'an to people, thus encouraging them to think about basic faith-related issues, such as the existence of God, His unity and the Hereafter, and to display the decrepit foundations and perverted works of godless systems.

Harun Yahya enjoys a wide readership in many countries, from India to America, England to Indonesia, Poland to Bosnia, and Spain to Brazil. Some of his books are available in English, French, German, Italian, Portuguese, Urdu, Arabic, Albanian, Russian, Serbo-Croat (Bosnian), Uygur Turkish, and Indonesian, and they have been enjoyed by readers all over the world.

Greatly appreciated all around the world, these works have been instrumental in many people putting their faith in God and in many others gaining a deeper insight into their faith. The wisdom, and the sincere and easy-to-understand style employed give these books a distinct touch which directly strikes any one who reads or examines them. Immune to objections, these works are characterised by their features of rapid effectiveness, definite results and irrefutability. It is unlikely that those who read these books and give a serious thought to them can any longer sincerely advocate the materialistic philosophy, atheism and any other perverted ideology or philosophy. Even if they continue to advocate, this will be only a sentimental insistence since these books have refuted these ideologies from their very basis. All contemporary movements of denial are ideologically defeated today, thanks to the collection of books written by Harun Yahya.

There is no doubt that these features result from the wisdom and lucidity of the Qur'an. The author certainly does not feel proud of himself; he merely intends to serve as a means in one's search for God's right path. Furthermore, no material gain is sought in the publication of these works.

Considering these facts, those who encourage people to read these books, which open the "eyes" of the heart and guide them in becoming more devoted servants of God, render an invaluable service.

Meanwhile, it would just be a waste of time and energy to propagate books which create confusion in peoples' minds, lead man into ideological chaos, and which, clearly have no strong and precise effects in removing the doubts in peoples' hearts, as also verified from previous experience. It is apparent that it is impossible for books devised to emphasize the author's literary power rather than the noble goal of saving people from loss of faith, to have such a great effect. Those who doubt this can readily see that the sole aim of Harun Yahya's books is to overcome disbelief and to disseminate the moral values of the Qur'an. The success, impact and sincerity this service has attained are manifest in the reader's conviction.

One point needs to be kept in mind: The main reason for the continuing cruelty and conflict, and all the ordeals Muslims undergo is the ideological prevalence of disbelief. These things can only come to an end with the ideological defeat of disbelief and by ensuring that everybody knows about the wonders of creation and Qur'anic morality, so that people can live by it. Considering the state of the world today, which forces people into the downward spiral of violence, corruption and conflict, it is clear that this service has to be provided more speedily and effectively. Otherwise, it may be too late.

It is no exaggeration to say that the collection of books by Harun Yahya have assumed this leading role. By the Will of God, these books will be the means through which people in the 21st century will attain the peace and bliss, justice and happiness promised in the Qur'an.

First published 2002
Reprinted 2003
© Goodword Books 2003

Goodword Books Pvt. Ltd.
1, Nizamuddin West Market, New Delhi-110013
Tel. (9111) 2435 5454, 2435 6666
Fax (9111) 2435 7333, 2435 7980
e-mail: info@goodwordbooks.com
Website: www.goodwordbooks.com

Printed in India

C O N T

E N T S

An Outdated View: The Theory of Evolution

Jean B. Lamarck: Science brought his theory down.

The idea that life is the product of an uncontrolled, purposeless process of coincidence is a 19th century myth. Looking at the matter from the primitive level of the science of the period, evolutionists assumed that life was very "simple".

There are more than a million species living on the earth. How did these creatures with entirely distinct features and perfect designs come into being? Anyone who uses his reason would understand that life is the work of a perfect and supreme creation.

However, the theory of evolution denies this explicit truth. It holds that all species on earth evolved from one another through a process based on random occurrences.

The first person to seriously take up the issue of evolution – an idea which originated in Ancient Greece – was the French biologist Jean Baptiste Lamarck. Lamarck's theory, which he postulated in the early 19th century, maintained that "living things transferred the traits they acquired during their lifetime to subsequent generations." In Lamarck's view, for instance, giraffes had evolved from antelope-like animals who extended their necks further and further as they tried to reach higher branches for food. The advent of the science of genetics, however, refuted Lamarck's theory once and for all.

The second important name to defend the theory after Lamarck was a British amateur naturalist, Charles Darwin. In his book *The Origin of Species*, published in 1856, he claimed that all species descended from a common ancestor through coincidences. According to Darwin, for instance, whales evolved from bears that tried to hunt in the sea.[1]

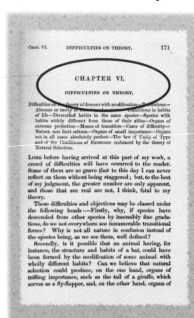

DARWIN'S DIFFICULTIES
Charles Darwin, an amateur naturalist, advanced his theory in his book, *The Origin of Species*, published in 1859. He confessed to many points which defied explanation in the chapter "Difficulties On Theory", and hoped that these problems would be solved in the future. This hope, however, came to nothing.

Darwin did not base his claim on any concrete evidence or finding. He just made some observations and produced some ideas. He carried out most of his observations on board a ship called the H.M.S. Beagle that had set sail from Britain.

Darwin had serious doubts as he put forward his assertions. He was not so confident of his theory. He confessed to there being many points which he was unable to explain in the chapter titled "Difficulties On Theory". Darwin had hoped that these problems would be solved in the future with the progress of science, and made some projections. 20th century science, however, disproved Darwin's claims one by one. The common point of Lamarck's and Darwin's theories was that both rested on a primitive understanding of science. The absence of various domains of science such as biochemistry and microbiology at the time led evolutionists to think that living things had a simple structure that could form by chance. Since the laws of genetics were not known, it was supposed that creatures could simply evolve into new species.

The progress of science overthrew all of these myths and revealed that living things are the work of a superior creation.

THE PRODUCT OF PRIMITIVE SCIENCE
When Darwin put forward his theory, not much was known about the finer details of living things. And with the primitive microscopes of the time, it was impossible to view the complex structures of life.

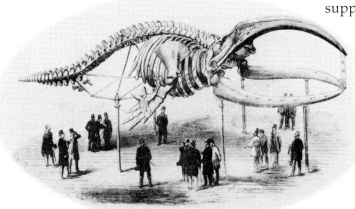

THE PROBLEM OF THE FOSSIL RECORD
When Darwin put forward his theory, palaeontologists opposed him the most. They knew that the "intermediary transitional forms" which Darwin imagined to have existed, never existed in reality. Darwin was hoping that this problem would be overcome by new fossil findings. Palaeontology, on the contrary, invalidated Darwin's theory more and more each day.

The Origin of Life

Evolutionists hold that living things spontaneously formed themselves from inanimate matter. However, this is a medieval superstition contradicting the main laws of biology.

DIVIDING CELLS
The most fundamental rule of life is the principle that "life comes only from life." A life form can originate only from another life form.

For many people, the question of "whether men descended from apes or not" springs to mind when Darwin's theory is mentioned. Before coming to that, however, there are numerous questions the evolutionary theory needs to answer. The first question is how the first living organism appeared on earth.

Evolutionists answer this question by saying that the first organism was a cell that emerged from inanimate matter by chance. According to the theory, at a time when the earth consisted of inanimate rocks, soil, gases and so on, a living organism formed by chance through the effects of wind, rain, and lightning. This evolutionary claim, however, is contrary to one of the most fundamental rules of biology: Life comes only from life, which means that inanimate matter cannot generate life.

The belief that inanimate matter can produce life is actually a medieval superstition. According to this theory, called "spontaneous generation", it was believed that mice sprang naturally from wheat, or maggots arose "spontaneously" from meat. At the time when Darwin put forward his theory, the belief that microbes of their own accord formed themselves from inanimate matter was also very common.

Louis Pasteur

"MUD THAT COMES TO LIFE"

The scientific name of the picture on the side is "Bathybius Haeckelii", that is, "Haeckel Mud". Ernst Haeckel, an ardent proponent of the theory of evolution, came to observe the mud dredged up by an exploratory vessel and thought that it closely resembled some cells he had seen under a microscope. Thus, he claimed that it is an inanimate material that turns into a living organism. Haeckel and his associate Darwin believed that life was simple enough to be formed out of inanimate material. 20th century science demonstrated, however, that life can never arise from lifelessness.

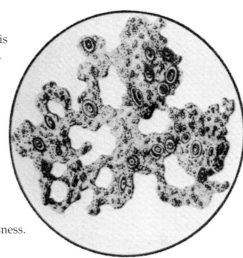

Ernst Haeckel

The findings of the French biologist Louis Pasteur put an end to this belief. As he put it: "The claim that inanimate matter can originate life is buried in history for good."[2] After Pasteur, evolutionists still maintained that the first living cell formed by chance. However, all experiments and research carried out throughout the 20th century ended in failure. The "chance" formation of a living cell aside, it has not even been possible to produce a living cell by a conscious process in the most advanced laboratories of the world.

Therefore, the question of how the first living organism emerged puts the evolutionary claim into a quandary right at the first step. One of the chief defenders of the theory of evolution at the molecular level, Prof. Jeffrey Bada, makes this confession:

Today as we leave the twentieth century, we still face the biggest unsolved problem that we had when we entered the twentieth century: How did life originate on Earth?[3]

While invalidating the theory of evolution, the law "life comes from life" also shows that the first life on earth came again from life, which means that it was created by God. He is the only One Who can give life to inanimate matter. In the words of the Qur'an, **"It is He Who brings out the living from the dead, and brings out the dead from the living."** (Surat ar-Rum: 19)

SPONTANEOUS GENERATION: A MEDIEVAL SUPERSTITION

One of the superstitious beliefs held by medieval people was that inanimate matter could spontaneously give rise to life. It was believed, for instance, that frogs and fish formed spontaneously from mud lying in riverbeds. It was later revealed that this hypothesis, known as "spontaneous generation", was simply a fallacy. However, though somewhat later and with a slightly different scenario, this belief was revived under the name of "the theory of evolution".

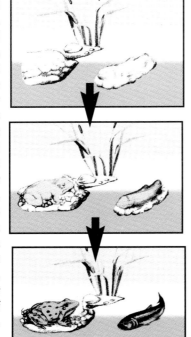

THE MYTH OF "CHEMICAL EVOLUTION"

Renowned evolutionist Alexander Oparin came up with the idea of "chemical evolution" at the beginning of the 20th century. This idea holds that the first living cell emerged by chance through some chemical reactions that took place in primordial earth conditions. However, no evolutionist, including Oparin, was able to submit any evidence to support the "chemical evolution" allegation. On the contrary, every new discovery in the 20th century showed that life was too complex to have originated by chance. Well-known evolutionist Leslie Orgel makes this admission: "(Examining the structures of DNA, RNA and proteins), one might have to conclude that life could never, in fact, have originated by chemical means."[4]

The Design in the Protein

Let us now put aside the question of "how the first cell originated" and ask a much easier question: How did the first protein originate? The theory of evolution has no answer to this question either.

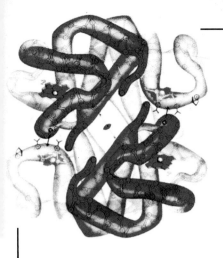

The complex design of the haemoglobin molecule

Proteins are the building blocks of the cell. If we compare the cell to a huge skyscraper, proteins are the bricks of the skyscraper. However, they do not have a standard form and structure as the bricks do. Even the simplest cells have roughly 2,000 different types of proteins. If cells can survive, it is thanks to the extraordinarily harmonious functioning of these distinct proteins.

Proteins are made up of smaller structures, or molecules, called "amino acids", which are formed by the different combinations made by carbon, nitrogen and hydrogen atoms. There are 500-1,000 amino acids in an average protein. Some proteins are much bigger.

The important point is that amino acids have to line up in a certain sequence to form a protein. There are 20 different amino acid types used in living organisms. These amino acids do not combine at random to form proteins. Every protein has a certain amino acid sequence and this sequence must be precisely matched. Even the deficiency or the replacement of a single amino acid renders that protein a useless lump of molecules. For this reason, every amino acid must be just at the right place in the right sequence. The instructions for this sequence are stored in the DNA of the cell and, according to them, the proteins are produced.

The theory of evolution claims that the first proteins formed "by chance". Probabilistic calculations, however, show that this is by no means possible.

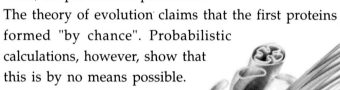

THE ARCHITECTURE IN PROTEINS
Besides having a sophisticated design, proteins are also involved in a great design in the body. The human body is mainly composed of proteins. Proteins are the basic material of our bones, eyes, hair or muscles. Here, you see the complex interior structure of a single fibre in one of our muscles. Cells with different protein make-ups form each of the details you see in this structure. Every detail is perfectly designed and built by the use of an organic material, which is protein. The fascinating architecture of proteins is one of the striking signs of creation.

PROTEIN SYNTHESIS

There is a continuous activity going on in our cells: the proteins in the food we eat are broken down and these pieces (amino acids) are re-combined according to the codes in DNA. Thus, new proteins needed by the body are made. This operation, called the protein synthesis, is far more complex than this simplified illustration. No laboratory is as successful as the cell in carrying protein synthesis.

Ribosome

Messenger RNA

Special enzymes

Elongating protein chain

Cell nucleus

Final shape of the protein

Protein chain bent by he enzymes

Re-processing of the protein chain

For instance, the probability of the amino acid sequence of a protein made up of 500 amino acids being in the correct order is 1 in 10^{950}.5 10^{950} is an incomprehensible figure formed by placing 950 zeros after 1. In mathematics, a probability smaller than 1 over 10^{50} is considered to be almost impossible.

Briefly, even a single protein cannot form by chance. Evolutionists also admit this fact from time to time. For instance, Harold Blum, a famous evolutionist scientist, states that "the spontaneous formation of a polypeptide of the size of the smallest known proteins seems beyond all probability."[6]

So, what does all this mean? Perry Reeves, a professor of chemistry, gives the answer:

> When one examines the vast number of possible structures that could result from a simple random combination of amino acids in an evaporating primordial pond, it is mind-boggling to believe that life could have originated in this way. It is more plausible that a Great Builder with a master plan would be required for such a task.[7]

CAN MONKEYS WRITE A BOOK?

Cytochrome-C is one of the most important proteins that make oxygen respiration possible. It is vital for survival. It is impossible for this protein, which has an extremely complex design, to form by chance. One of the foremost defenders of evolution in Turkey, Professor Ali Demirsoy states in his book Inheritance and Evolution that the probability of the coincidental formation of Cytochrome-C is "as unlikely as the possibility of a monkey writing the history of humanity on a typewriter without making any mistakes."[8]

Cytochrome-C protein

The Design in the Cell

All living things are made up of cells. Even a single cell is self-sufficient; it can produce its own food, move, and communicate with other cells. With its extraordinary technology, the cell is concrete evidence that life cannot originate by chance.

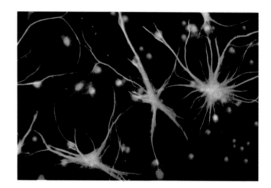

THE COMPLEXITY OF THE BRAIN CELL
A brain cell is in constant interaction with others numbering up to 10,000. This communication network is far more complex than all the switchboards in the world.

The cell, even a single protein of which cannot form by chance, is a wonder of design that renders the "chance" hypothesis of evolution completely meaningless. In the cell, there are power stations, complex factories, a huge data bank, storage systems, and advanced refineries.

In Darwin's time, nothing was known about the extraordinary structure of the cell. Under the primitive microscopes of the day, the cell seemed to be a murky lump. For this reason, both Darwin and other evolutionists of his time believed that a cell was a simple driblet of water that could easily originate by chance. The idea that life could be

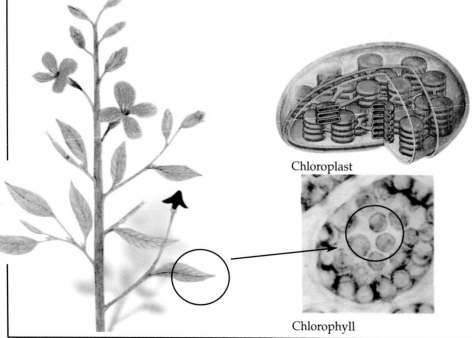

Chloroplast

Chlorophyll

PLANT CELL
In addition to human and animal cells, the plant cell, too, is a miracle of creation. The plant cell carries out a process that no laboratory is able to perform today: "photosynthesis." An organelle called "chloroplast" in the plant cell enables plants to produce starch by using water, carbon dioxide, and sunlight. This substance is the first link of the food chain on the Earth and the food source of all living things. The details of this highly complex process are still unknown today.

attributed to chance gained acceptance because of this primitive scientific view.

The scientific developments in the 20th century, however, revealed that the cell has an unimaginably complex system. Today, it is established that the cell, which has such a complex design, could not possibly originate by chance as the theory of evolution claims. It is certain that a structure too complex to be imitated even by man cannot be the work of "chance". Renowned British mathematician and astronomer Professor Fred Hoyle puts this impossibility like this:

> *The chance that higher life forms might have emerged in this way is comparable with the chance that a tornado sweeping through a junk-yard might assemble a Boeing 747 from the materials therein.*[9]

And in another commentary, Hoyle says: "Indeed, such a theory (that life was assembled by an intelligence) is so obvious that one wonders why it is not widely accepted as being self-evident. The reasons are psychological rather than scientific."[10]

An immunity cell capturing the germs that have entered the body.

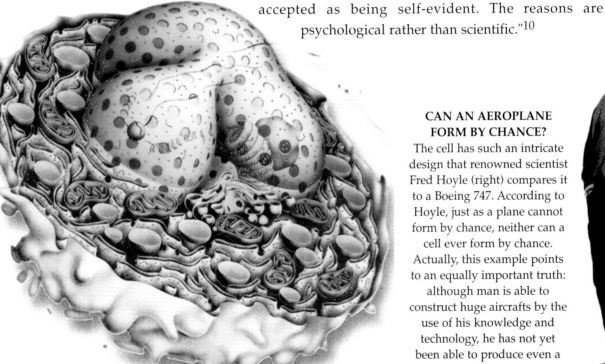

CAN AN AEROPLANE FORM BY CHANCE?

The cell has such an intricate design that renowned scientist Fred Hoyle (right) compares it to a Boeing 747. According to Hoyle, just as a plane cannot form by chance, neither can a cell ever form by chance. Actually, this example points to an equally important truth: although man is able to construct huge aircrafts by the use of his knowledge and technology, he has not yet been able to produce even a single cell.

Genetic Information

Did you know that the nucleus of each of the trillions of cells making up the human body includes a data bank big enough to fill a 900-volume encyclopaedia?

DNA is a huge molecule hidden in the nucleus of every living cell. All physical traits of a creature are coded in this helical molecule. All the information about our bodies, from the colour of our eyes to the structure of our internal organs and the form and functions of our cells, are encoded in sections called genes in DNA.

The DNA code is made up of the sequence of four different bases. If we think of each of these bases as a letter, DNA can be likened to a databank made up of an alphabet of four letters. All the information about a living thing is stored in this databank.

If we attempted to write down the information in DNA, this would take up approximately a million pages. This is equal to an encyclopaedia forty times bigger than *The Encyclopaedia Britannica,* which is one of mankind's greatest accumulations of information. This incredible information is stored in the tiny nucleus of our cells measuring about a thousandth of a millimeter in size.

It is calculated that a DNA chain small enough to fill a teaspoon has the capacity to store all the information contained in all the books ever written.

Of course, such an amazing structure could never have been formed by chance and this proves that life is created by God. Not surprisingly, evolutionists are unable to bring any explanation to the origin of DNA.

The structure of DNA was discovered by two scientists named Francis Crick and James Watson. Despite being an evolutionist, Crick said that DNA could never have emerged by coincidence.

REPLICATION MIRACLE

If you leave a bacterium in a suitable environment, in a few hours you will see that it has produced hundreds of copies of similar bacteria. Every living cell has the ability to "copy itself".

Until the discovery of DNA, how this miraculous process took place was unknown. With the discovery of DNA, it was revealed that every living cell has a "data bank" that stores all the information about itself. This discovery displayed the wonder of creation.

DNA includes not only the plan of cells, but also the complete body plan of living things. The structure of our internal organs, or the shape of a bird's wings, in short, everything is encoded in DNA down to its smallest details.

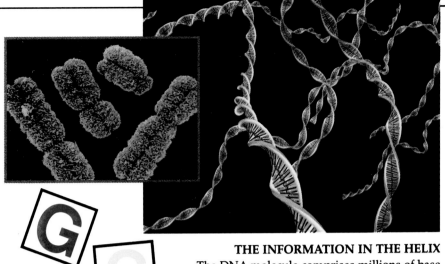

THE INFORMATION IN THE HELIX
The DNA molecule comprises millions of base pairs organized in a helical shape. If a DNA molecule in only one of our cells were unfolded, it would make a one-metre long chain. This chain, squeezed into the cell nucleus, is only as big as a hundred thousandth of a millimeter with an amazing "packaging" system.

DNA has an alphabet with four "letters".

However, they still embrace the "chance" hypothesis simply for the sake of keeping the theory alive. A well-known molecular biologist from Australia, Michael Denton, explains this in his book *Evolution: A Theory in Crisis*:

> *To the skeptic, the proposition that the genetic programmes of higher organisms, consisting of something close to a thousand million bits of information, equivalent to the sequence of letters in a small library of one thousand volumes, containing in encoded form countless thousands of intricate algorithms controlling, specifying, and ordering the growth and development of billions and billions of cells into the form of a complex organism, were composed by a purely random process is simply an affront to reason. But to the Darwinist, the idea is accepted without a ripple of doubt - the paradigm takes precedence!*[11]

The biochemical make-up of a wolf's fur, its thickness, colour or the angle at which it grows are encoded in its DNA

Every piece of information is derived from an intelligent source that brings it into being. The fascinating information in DNA is evidence of the supreme wisdom and creative power of God.

The Design in Nature

The fact that living things have perfectly designed forms proves that they could never have originated by chance. The design in nature is a clear sign of creation.

This is not the head of a snake but the tail of a caterpillar! In a moment of danger, the caterpillar puffs up its tail which is designed to look exactly like a snake's head and intimidates its enemies.

What would you think if you went out trekking in the depths of a thick forest and ran across a latest-model car among the trees? Would you think that various elements in the forest had come together by chance over millions of years and produced such a vehicle? All the raw materials making up the car are obtained from iron, plastic, rubber, earth or its by-products, but would this fact lead you to think that these materials had come together "by chance" and had, by themselves, manufactured such a car?

Without doubt, anyone with a sound mind would know that the car was the product of an intelligent design, that is, it was factory-made, and would wonder what it was doing there in the middle of a jungle. The sudden origination of a complex structure in a complete form out of the blue shows that it is made by an intelligent agent.

The example of the car also holds true for living things. In fact, the design in life is too striking to be compared to that in a car. The cell, the basic unit of life, is far more complex than any man-made technological product. Moreover, this irreducibly complex organism must have emerged suddenly and fully formed.

Therefore, it is crystal clear that all living things are the work of a superior "design". To put it more clearly, there is no doubt that all creatures are created by God.

In the face of this explicit truth, evolutionists resort to a single concept: "chance". By believing that pure chance can produce perfect designs, evolutionists cross the bounds of reason and science. The famous zoologist Pierre Grassé, the former president of the French Academy of Sciences, makes his point about the logic of "chance", which is the backbone of Darwinism:

> The opportune appearance of mutations permitting animals and plants to meet their needs seems hard to believe. Yet the Darwinian theory is even more demanding: A single plant, a single animal

This fish is created with a very interesting hunting system. It keeps this system undisclosed under normal conditions.

When it sees its prey, it opens its upper fin. This fin is designed just like a small fish down to its smallest details.

1

2

THE DESIGN IN OUR HANDS

The human hand has a perfect design that gives us ideal movement ability. Each one of the 27 small bones making up the hand is positioned properly with a certain engineering calculation. The muscles that help us to move our fingers are located in our lower arms so as not to make our hands clumsy. These muscles are connected by strong tendons to three small bones in our fingers. Moreover, there is a special bracelet-like tissue in our wrists that fastens all these tendons. The hand has such a perfect design that no "robot hand" produced by modern technology has been able to imitate the abilities of the hand.

would require thousands and thousands of lucky, appropriate events. Thus, miracles would become the rule: events with an infinitesimal probability could not fail to occur… There is no law against daydreaming, but science must not indulge in it.[12]

Grassé summarises what the concept of "coincidence" means for evolutionists: "...Chance becomes a sort of providence, which, under the cover of atheism, is not named but which is secretly worshipped."[13]

This is the type of superstition that underlies Darwinism.

BONE AND THE EIFFEL TOWER

Examples of design in nature often become a source of inspiration for technological designs. An example is the spongy structure of the human bone furnished with small tendons, which inspired the famous Eiffel Tower in Paris. This structure is responsible for the strength, elasticity, and lightness of bones. The same properties also exist in the Eiffel Tower, though not as effectively as in bones.

A PERFECT HUNTER: THE VENUS' FLYTRAP

A carnivorous plant, the Venus' Flytrap, is a perfect hunter that swiftly catches the flies landing on it. It is impossible for this trap system working with electric signals to be the work of coincidence or a gradual developmental process. The perfect design of the Venus' flytrap is one of the numerous signs of creation.

The prey, lured by the fake fish, draws near and suddenly falls a victim to it.

3

Miller's Experiment

Evolutionists often quote Miller's Experiment as evidence of the correctness of their claim that life formed by chance in primordial earth conditions. However, the experiment, which was carried out some 50 years ago, has lost its scientific implication due to the discoveries that followed.

Miller with his experiment apparatus

American chemist Stanley Miller conducted an experiment in 1953 to support the scenario of molecular evolution. Miller assumed that the primordial earth atmosphere was composed of methane, ammonia, and hydrogen gases. He combined these gases in an experiment set-up and gave electricity to the mixture. Almost a week later, he observed that some amino acids formed in this mixture.

This discovery aroused great excitement among evolutionists. In the next twenty years, some evolutionists, such as Sydney Fox and Cyril Ponnamperuma, attempted to develop Miller's scenario.

The discoveries made in the 1970's repudiated these evolutionist attempts known as "primordial atmosphere experiments". It was revealed that the "methane-ammonia based primordial atmosphere model" Miller proposed and other evolutionists accepted was absolutely fallacious. Miller chose these gases on purpose, because they were very convenient for the formation of amino acids. Scientific discoveries, on the other hand, showed that the primordial atmosphere was composed of nitrogen, carbon dioxide and water vapour.[14] This atmosphere model was by no means suitable for the formation of amino acids. Moreover, it was understood that a great amount of oxygen naturally occurred in the primordial atmosphere.[15] This, too, invalidated the scenario of the evolutionists, because free oxygen would obviously decompose amino acids.

As a result of these discoveries, the scientific community acknowledged in the

PRIMORDIAL ATMOSPHERE MISCONCEPTION
Miller claimed that he strictly reproduced the primordial atmosphere conditions in his experiment. However, the gases Miller used in his experiment were not even remotely comparable to the real primordial earth conditions. Moreover, Miller had interfered in the experiment with purposeful mechanisms. In fact, with this experiment, he himself refuted the evolutionist claims that amino acids could have formed spontaneously in natural conditions.

MILLER'S ASSUMPTIONS	REAL CONDITIONS	WHY IS THE EXPERIMENT INVALID?
He used methane, ammonia, and water vapour in the experiment.	Primitive earth contained carbon dioxide and nitrogen instead of methane and ammonia.	Ferris and Chen from the USA repeated the experiment with the gases that existed at that time. Not even one amino acid was obtained.
He assumed oxygen to be non-existent in the primitive atmosphere.	Findings show that there was a huge amount of free oxygen in the primitive atmosphere.	With such an amount of free oxygen available, the amino acids would have broken down, even if they could have been formed.
There was a special mechanism set up to synthesize the amino acids in the experiment. This mechanism, called the "Cold Trap", isolated the amino acids from the environment as soon as they were formed and preserved them.	It was impossible for these kinds of mechanisms to have existed in nature. Under natural conditions, amino acids are exposed to all kinds of external destructive factors.	If the mechanism known as the "Cold Trap" had not existed, the spark source and other chemicals released during the experiment would have destroyed the amino acids.

1980's that Miller's Experiment and other "primordial atmosphere experiments" that followed it have no meaning at all. After a long silence, Miller also confessed that the atmosphere medium he used was unrealistic.[16]

What's more, this whole fuss was simply about "amino acid formation". Even if amino acids had formed, it is impossible for these simple organic molecules to give rise to extremely complex structures such as proteins by chance and produce a living cell which even mankind is unable to reproduce in laboratories today.

The fifty years that have passed since Miller's time have only served to further display the despair the theory of evolution faces at the molecular level.

MILLER'S CONFESSION:
Today, Miller too accepts that his 1953 experiment was very far from explaining the origin of life.

FOX'S UNSUCCESSFUL EXPERIMENT
Inspired by Miller's scenario, evolutionists conducted different experiments in the years that followed. Sydney Fox produced the molecules seen in the picture, "proteinoids" as he called them, by combining some amino acids. These useless amino acid chains had nothing to do with real proteins that constitute the bodies of living things. Actually, all these efforts not only showed that life did not come about by coincidence, but also that it could not be reproduced in laboratory conditions.

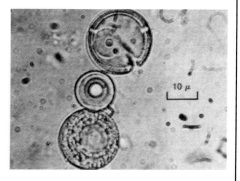

10 μ

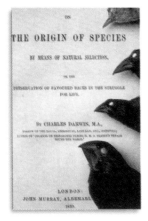

Darwin's book: *The Origin of Species, By Means of Natural Selection…*

The Natural Selection Misconception

Natural selection, which Darwin proposed as an evolutionary mechanism, has in fact no evolutionary power. Natural selection cannot form new species.

J ust as it is impossible for life to arise on earth by chance, so is it for species to transform themselves into other species. For no such power exists in nature. What we call nature is the sum of unconscious atoms that make up the soil, rocks, air, water, and everything else. This lifeless heap of matter has no power to transform an invertebrate creature into a fish, then make it climb on land and turn into a reptile, and then turn it into a bird and make it fly, and finally make it a human.

Claiming just the opposite, Darwin put forward a single concept as an "evolutionary mechanism": Natural Selection. Natural selection centres around the idea that the strongest creatures that are best fitted to their habitat will survive. For instance, in a deer herd threatened by wild animals, those that can run faster

THE EFFECT OF LAMARCK:
When Darwin suggested that "natural selection causes species to evolve", he was inspired by Lamarck's hypothesis about the "transfer of acquired traits". According to Lamarck, the necks of giraffes extended as they tried to reach higher branches for food. In the 20th century, however, it was revealed that Lamarckism is a fallacy.

SELECTION CANNOT FORM A NEW SPECIES
In nature, weak individuals are eliminated and replaced by stronger ones. This phenomenon, however, does not cause new species to emerge. Even if wild animals hunt weak and slow-moving deer for billions of years, deer will never turn into a different species.

Dark and light coloured moths already existed both before and after the industrial revolution. A new moth species did not emerge.

BEFORE THE REVOLUTION   AFTER THE REVOLUTION

THE STORY OF INDUSTRIAL MELANISM

Evolutionists commonly quote the "Moths of the Industrial Revolution" in 18th century England as an "observed example of evolution through natural selection". According to the account, around the outset of the Industrial Revolution in England, the colour of the tree barks around Manchester was quite light. Since dark-coloured moths resting on those trees could readily be noticed, they fell easy prey to the birds and therefore, were rare. Yet when the barks of the trees darkened as a result of pollution caused by the industrial revolution, this time

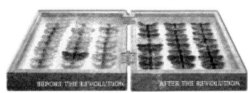

Moth collection showing that both dark-coloured and light-coloured moths lived in the region before the industrial revolution.

the light-coloured moths became the most hunted and the number of dark-coloured moths increased. This is not an example of "evolution", because natural selection did not give rise to a species that did not exist in nature earlier. Dark-coloured moths were already extant before the industrial revolution. Here, we see the moths collected by a moth collector before and after the industrial revolution. There is only a shift in the number of existing moth species. Moths did not acquire a new organ or feature to lead to a "change in their species".

will survive. Yet certainly, this mechanism would not cause deer to evolve – it would not transform them into another living species, for instance, elephants.

There is not a single shred of observational evidence showing that natural selection has ever caused any living thing to evolve. A noted evolutionist, British paleontologist Colin Patterson confesses this fact:

No one has ever produced a species by mechanisms of natural selection. No one has ever got near it and most of the current argument in neo-Darwinism is about this question.[17]

SACRIFICE IN ANIMALS
Darwin's theory of evolution by means of natural selection rested on the supposition that all living things fight a fierce struggle for survival.

Observations however showed that animal communities display great examples of self-sacrifice and cooperation. The wild oxen that line up in a circle to protect their young are only one of the numerous instances of self-sacrifice in nature.

Mutations

Mutations are genetic accidents that occur in living things. Like all accidents, they cause harm and destruction. "Evolution" through mutation is as unlikely as the improvement of a clock by a hammer blow.

Realizing that natural selection has no evolutionary function, evolutionists introduced the concept of "mutation" to their claim in the 20th century. Mutations are distortions taking place in the genes of organisms through external effects such as radiation. Evolutionists claim that these distortions cause organisms to evolve.

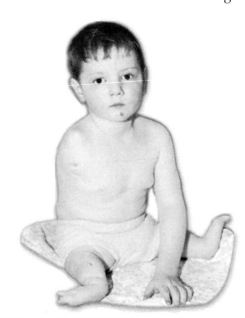

Scientific findings, however, reject this claim, because all observable efficient mutations cause only harm to living things. All mutations that take place in humans result in mental or physical deformities such as mongolism (Down's syndrome), albinism, dwarfism, or diseases such as cancer.

Another reason why it is impossible for mutations to cause living things to evolve is that mutations do not add any new genetic information to an organism. Mutations cause existing genetic information to be randomly reshuffled similar to playing cards. In other words, no new genetic information is introduced by mutations.

Evolutionary theory, however, asserts that the genetic information of living things increases over time. For instance, while a very simply structured bacterium comprises of 2,000 different types of proteins, a human's organism has 100,000 types of proteins. Exactly 98,000 new proteins have to be "discovered" for a bacterium to evolve into a human being.

EFFECTS OF CHERNOBYL
The main cause of mutation in humans is radioactivity. The effects of mutations are always detrimental. Those who were exposed to mutation because of the disaster in Chernobyl either suffered from fatal cancers or were born with crippled organs as seen in the pictures.

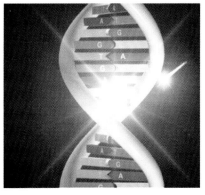
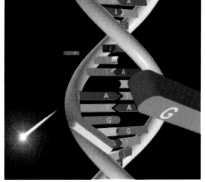

THE DISTORTION OF DNA
The code in DNA determines the physical traits of living things. If a displacement or relocation occurs in this code, because of an external effect like radiation, the organism mutates.

It is by no means possible for these protein structures to be produced by mutations, because mutations cannot add anything to a DNA chain.

Not surprisingly, so far, not even a single mutation has been observed to develop the genetic information of any life form. Despite being an evolutionist himself, the Former President of the French Academy of Sciences, Pierre-Paul Grassé, made the following admission: "No matter how numerous they may be, mutations do not produce any kind of evolution."[18]

THE MISTAKE OF DE VRIES
The Dutch botanist Hugh de Vries, who discovered the mutation mechanism, thought that he had found an "evolutionary mechanism". Experiments and observations over the years, however, showed that mutations are merely "distortion mechanisms".

MUTATION TWINS
The disorder resulting in "Siamese twins" in humans is caused by mutations. These twin frogs which were conjoined at birth give us an idea of the results of mutation.

FRUIT FLY EXPERIMENTS
For decades, evolutionists carried out mutation experiments on fruit flies because they reproduce very rapidly and can be easily mutated. These creatures were mutated millions of times in all possible ways. However, not even one beneficial mutation has been observed.

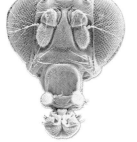

The head of a fruit fly before it is mutated

Result of mutation: Legs jutting from the head

Irreducible Complexity

All claims of Darwinism rest on the scenario of "gradual development". The "irreducibly complex" organs unravelled by 20th century science demolish this scenario and the entire theory of evolution along with it.

In order for a watch to function, all of its wheels must exist. Even if there is one missing wheel, the watch will be useless. This "irreducibly complex" structure shows that the watch is a work of perfection made by a designer of superior skills.

If you ask an evolutionist: "How did the marvellous organs of living things come into being?", he will outline this scenario: "It is true that the extremely complex systems of living organisms cannot form all of a sudden by chance. These systems have rather developed step by step. First, a single part of the system emerged by chance. Since this part was advantageous for the organism, that organism benefited from natural selection. Then other parts formed by steps, eventually building the highly complex system."

The point that renders this scenario invalid right from the outset is the characteristic of "irreducible complexity" in the systems of living things. If a system is not functional without all of its components being in place, and if it is useless if even only one of its components is missing, then that system cannot be reduced to a simpler form. It either exists perfectly and functions, or it is useless.

On close consideration, we see that an "irreducibly complex" system cannot possibly form "step by step" through coincidences. For no "intermediate step" would be of any use unless the system were complete and perfect. A useless intermediate step, on the other hand, would be eliminated by natural selection and disappear according to the reasoning of evolution.

When Darwin put forward his theory, he had great doubts about this point. He imagined that the organs of living things could be reduced to simpler forms, yet he was also afraid that new developments would destroy his speculation. This is why he wrote the following lines in his book *The Origin of Species*:

If it could be demonstrated that any complex organ existed, which could not

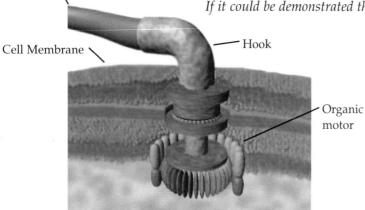

Filament

Cell Membrane

Hook

Organic motor

BACTERIAL FLAGELLUM

This complicated structure is an electric motor. But not one in a household appliance or vehicle. It is in a bacterium. Thanks to this motor, bacteria have been able to move those organs known as "flagella" and thus swim in water for millions of years. The motor of bacteria flagellum, discovered in the 1970's, staggered the scientific community, because this "irreducibly complex" organ, made up of some 250 separate molecular components, can never be explained by chance mechanisms as Darwin had proposed.

THE DESIGN OF THE EYE

The human eye works by some 40 different parts functioning together. If one of these is not present, the eye will serve no purpose. Each of these 40 parts has its own individual structure. For instance, the retinal membrane at the back of the eye is made up of 11 different layers. (Right below) One of these layers is the blood vein network, as seen under a microscope. (See side picture.) This layer, which has the most intricate vein network in the body, meets the oxygen needs of the retinal cells that interpret light. Each of the other layers has a distinct function. Evolutionists are unable to account for the development of such a complex organ.

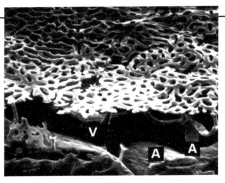

One of the 11 distinct layers of the retinal membrane.

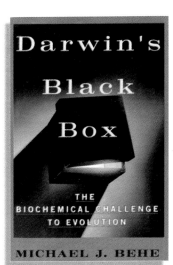

The cross section of the retina

possibly have been formed by numerous, successive, slight modifications, my theory would absolutely break down.[19]

Darwin's theory has today been overthrown just as he feared, because scientific findings prove that most of the systems in living organisms are irreducibly complex. Numerous structures and systems from the human eye to the cell, from the coagulation process in the blood to the protein, are of no use with even one of their components missing. Not surprisingly, no evolutionist can explain through which "steps" these organisms have formed.

While irreducible complexity – in Darwin's words – "absolutely" breaks down the theory of evolution, it, on the other hand, absolutely proves creation. Every irreducibly complex system demonstrates the existence of an intelligence that has built it. The complexity in living things proves the existence and the perfect creation of God, Who created life. As stated in the Qur'an, **"He is God – the Creator, the Maker, the Giver of Form. To Him belong the Most Beautiful Names. Everything in the heavens and earth glorifies Him. He is the Almighty, the All-Wise." (Surat al-Hashr: 24)**

THE BIOCHEMICAL CHALLENGE TO EVOLUTION

In his book *Darwin's Black Box: The Biochemical Challenge to Evolution*, the American professor of biochemistry, Michael Behe, quotes many examples of irreducible complexity. As Behe makes clear, while irreducibly complex organs refute Darwinism, they prove, on the other hand, that life is "designed" that is, it is created.

Impasse of Intermediate Forms

Darwin had written: "If my theory be true, numberless intermediate varieties... must assuredly have existed". However, evolutionists, despite their 140 year-long search, have not been able to find even one.

Darwin admitted the non-existence of intermediate form fossils in the chapter titled "Imperfection of Geological Record" of his book *The Origin of Species*.

In the excavations carried out from Darwin's time till the present day, not even one intermediate form has been unearthed.

The theory of evolution asserts that living things descended from a common ancestor. According to the theory, living beings differentiated from each other over a very long time with linked, gradual modifications.

If this assertion were true, then numerous "intermediary species" should have lived in history linking different living species. For instance, if birds had indeed evolved from reptiles, then billions of creatures which were half-bird/half-reptile should have lived throughout history.

Darwin knew that the fossil deposits ought to be full of these "intermediary transitional forms". Yet he was also well aware that no transitional form fossils were available. That was why he devoted a chapter to this problem in his book *The Origin of Species*.

Darwin was hoping that this great problem would be solved in the future and that transitional forms would be discovered with new excavations. Despite their best efforts, however, evolutionists have not been able to find even a single intermediate form in the 140 years that have passed since Darwin. The well-known evolutionist Derek Ager confesses this fact:

> *The point emerges that if we examine the fossil record in detail, we find—over and over again—not gradual evolution, but the sudden explosion of one group at the expense of another.*[20]

"MOSAIC" ORGANISMS ARE NOT INTERMEDIATE FORMS

The most important example of evolutionists' alleged intermediate forms is a fossil bird called *Archaeopteryx*. Focusing on the teeth and claws of *Archaeopteryx*, evolutionists allege that this creature is an intermediate form between reptiles and birds.

However, an animal class may well possess features of another animal class, without this being an indication that it is a transitional form. For instance, the Australian platypus reproduces by laying eggs like reptiles despite being a mammal. Besides, it has a beak similar to a bird's. Scientists call organisms like platypus "mosaic forms". Leading evolutionists now also admit that mosaic forms cannot be considered as intermediate forms.

The sudden origination of living beings on the Earth is proof that they were created by God. Evolutionist biologist Douglas Futuyma admits this fact:

> Organisms either appeared on the earth fully developed or they did not. If they did not, they must have developed from preexisting species by some process of modification. If they did appear in a fully developed state, they must indeed have been created by some omnipotent intelligence.[21]

SIMILAR CREATURES ARE NOT INTERMEDIATE FORMS

The fact that similar animals in different sizes have been found throughout the ages is not evidence for there being "intermediate forms". If the different deer and gazelle species we see in the picture had been available only as fossil forms, evolutionists might well have made an imaginary evolutionary scheme by arranging them in a line progressing from the smallest to the biggest. Yet, these animals are not intermediate forms, but individual living species.

INTERMEDIATE FORMS MUST BE "HALF" ORGANISMS

The intermediate forms evolutionists have to find are organisms that are in between two species and that have missing and half developed organs. For instance, if invertebrates like starfish had evolved into fish as evolutionists claim, many "half fish" and "half starfish" organisms ought to have lived. In the fossil record, however, there are only perfect starfish and perfect fish.

IMAGINARY CREATURES

The imaginary transitional forms existing in the fantasy of evolutionists ought to have missing and defective organs. For instance, a creature in between birds and reptiles would have half wings and half avian lungs. However, no fossil of such a creature has yet been found, as it is not possible for such a "weird" creature as we see in the picture to survive. All fossils that are discovered belong to complete and perfectly designed creatures.

The Cambrian Period

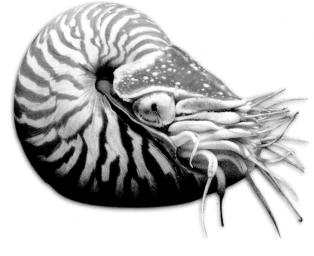

When we examine the earth strata, we see that life on Earth appeared suddenly. Many diverse living species emerged abruptly and fully in the Cambrian Period. This finding is compelling evidence for creation.

A still extant example of the Cambrian Period: *Nautilus*

The deepest stratum of earth that contains fossils of complex living things is the "Cambrian", which has an estimated age of 520 to 530 million years. The fossils unearthed in Cambrian rocks belonged to complex invertebrate species like snails, trilobites, sponges, worms, jelly fish, starfish, crustaceans and sea lilies. Most interestingly, all of these distinct species emerged all of a sudden without any predecessor.

Richard Monastersky, the editor of *Earth Sciences*, which is one of the popular journals of evolutionist literature, admits this fact that put evolutionists into a quandary:

> *A half-billion years ago the remarkably complex forms of animals that we see today suddenly appeared. This moment, right at the start of the earth's Cambrian Period, some 550 million years ago, marks the evolutionary explosion that filled the seas with the earth's first complex creatures. The large animal phyla of today were present already in the early Cambrian and they were as distinct from each other as they are today.*[22]

How these distinct living species with no common ancestors could have emerged is a question that remains unanswered by evolutionists. The Oxford zoologist Richard Dawkins, one of the foremost advocates of the evolutionary theory in the world, makes this confession:

COMPLEX SYSTEMS
Most of the life forms that emerged all of a sudden in the Cambrian Period had complex systems like eyes, gills, circulatory system, and advanced physiological structures no different from their modern counterparts.

An illustration of the organisms that existed in the Cambrian Period

It is as though they (the species of the Cambrian) were just planted there, without any evolutionary history.[23]

The Cambrian explosion is clear evidence that God created all living things. The only explanation of the sudden emergence of organisms without any evolutionary ancestors is creation. Accordingly, Darwin wrote: "If numerous species, belonging to the same genera or families, have really started into life all at once, the fact would be fatal to the theory of descent with slow modification through natural selection."[24]

This fatal stroke that frightened Darwin comes from the Cambrian period, right at the outset of the fossil record.

THE EYE OF THE TRILOBITE

The eye of the trilobite, one of the species of the Cambrian, had an extraordinary design. It consisted of hundreds of tiny eyes. Moreover, each of these tiny eyes had two different lenses. It is reckoned that this structure called the "doublet structure" allowed the trilobites to see underwater perfectly, without distortion. A professor of geology from the University of Harvard, David Raup says: "The trilobites used an optimal design which would require a well trained and imaginative optical engineer to develop today."[25]

This perfect eye structure was brought into being 530 million years ago all of a sudden in its perfect form. Additionally, the compound eye system of the trilobites has survived to our day without a single alteration. Some insects, such as bees and dragon-flies, have the same eye structure as did the trilobite.

The compound eye structure of the trilobite

Fish and Amphibians

Fish and amphibians emerged on the Earth suddenly and without any predecessors. Evolutionists cannot explain the origin of either of these living classes.

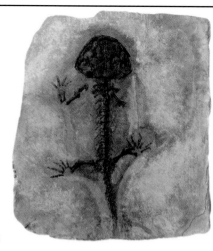

E volutionists assume that the sea invertebrates that appeared in the Cambrian stratum somehow evolved into fish over tens of millions of years. However, there is not a single transitional link indicating that evolution occurred between these invertebrates and fish. Actually, the evolution of invertebrates that have their hard tissues outside their bodies and no skeleton into bony fish that have theirs in the middle of their bodies is a very big transformation which should have left a great number of transitional links.

Evolutionists have been digging fossil strata for about 140 years looking for these hypothetical forms. They have found millions of invertebrate fossils and millions of fish fossils; yet nobody has ever found even one that is midway between them.

An evolutionist paleontologist, Gerald T. Todd, asks the following questions in the face of this fact:

> *All three subdivisions of the bony fishes first appear in the fossil record at approximately the same time… How did they originate? What allowed them to diverge so widely?.. And why is there no trace of earlier, intermediate forms?*[26]

The evolutionary scenario also argues that fish, which evolved from invertebrates, later transformed themselves into amphibians which are able to live on land. (Amphibians are animals capable of living both on land and in water, such as frogs.) But as you would imagine, this scenario also lacks evidence. There is not even a single fossil verifying that a half-fish/half-amphibian creature has ever existed. This fact is confirmed, albeit reluctantly, by a well-known evolutionist authority, Robert L. Carroll, who is the author of *Vertebrate Paleontology and Evolution*: "We have no intermediate fossils between rhipidistian fish and early amphibians."[27]

In short, both fish and amphibians emerged suddenly and in their present form without any predecessors. In other words, God created them in a perfect form.

A fossil dating back 280 million years belonging to an extinct frog species. These discoveries reveal that frogs appeared suddenly on the Earth without any predecessors.

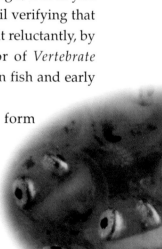

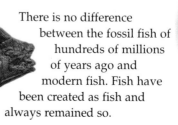

There is no difference between the fossil fish of hundreds of millions of years ago and modern fish. Fish have been created as fish and always remained so.

M

Reptile

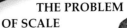

THE PROBLEM OF SCALE

One of the important contradictions in the fanciful evolutionary scheme stretching from fish to reptiles is the skin formation of these organisms. All fish have scales on their skin while amphibians do not. Reptiles that have allegedly evolved from amphibians also have scales. If we suppose that there is an evolutionary relationship between these organisms, we also have to answer why scales, which exist in fish, disappeared in amphibians, and then re-appeared in reptiles.

Evolutionists, however, are unable to answer this question.

Amphibian

Fish

THE MIRACLE OF METAMORPHOSIS

Frogs are first born in water, live there for a while, and then emerge on to land in a process known as "metamorphosis." Some people think that metamorphosis is evidence of evolution, whereas, the two have actually nothing to do with one another. The sole development mechanism proposed by evolution is mutation. Metamorphosis does not come about by coincidental effects as mutation does. On the contrary, this change results from the frogs' genetic code. In other words, it is already evident that when a frog is first born, it will have a type of body allowing it to live on land. The evolutionists' claim of passage from water to land says that fish, with a genetic code completely designed to allow them to live in water, turned into land creatures as a result of chance mutations. But for this reason, metamorphosis actually tears evolution down, rather than shoring it up. Because the slightest error in the process of metamorphosis means the creature will die or be deformed. It is essential that metamorphosis should happen perfectly. It is impossible for such a complex process, which allows no room for error, to have come about by chance mutations, as is claimed by evolution. Metamorphosis is actually a miracle that reveals the perfection in creation.

With metamorphosis, frogs alter in form. At the end of a perfect transformation, they become adapted to live on land.

The offspring that will emerge from the fertilized frog eggs will be plentiful enough to cover a lake or a flowing river.

The frog offspring hatching from its egg is a fish-like organism designed to live in water prior to metamorphosis. It takes in oxygen through gills just as fish do. Frogs at this stage are called "tadpoles".

Coelacanth Misconception

Up until 70 years ago, evolutionists had a fossil fish which they considered "the ancestor of land animals". Scientific developments, however, put an end to all evolutionist claims about this fish.

The absence of intermediate form fossils between fish and amphibians is a fact evolutionists also admit to today. However, until 70 years ago, it was accepted that a fossil fish called the coelacanth was an outright intermediate form. Evolutionists claimed that the coelacanth, which was estimated to be 410 million years of age, was a transitional form with a primitive lung, a developed brain, a digestive and a circulatory system ready to function on land, and even a primitive walking mechanism. These evolutionary interpretations were accepted as undisputed truth in scientific circles until the end of the 1930's.

However, on December 22, 1938, a very interesting discovery was made in the Indian Ocean. A living member of the coelacanth family, previously presented as a transitional form that had become extinct 70 million years ago, was caught! The discovery of a "living" prototype of coelacanth undoubtedly gave evolutionists a severe shock. The evolutionist paleontologist, J.L.B. Smith, said that he could not have been more surprised if he had come across a living dinosaur.[28] In the following years, more than 200 coelacanths were caught in different parts of the world.

Living coelacanths revealed how far evolutionists could go in making up their imaginary scenarios. Contrary to their claims, coelacanths had neither a primitive lung nor a large brain. The organ that evolutionist researchers claimed to be a primitive lung turned out

IMAGINARY DRAWINGS AND A REAL COELACANTH
Until a living specimen of it was found, evolutionists presented the coelacanth as the ancestor of "all land animals". Drawings such as the above were presented as fact and took their place in textbooks. When a living example of the fish was caught (side picture), all these evolutionist allegations were debunked.

EVOLUTIONIST PREMISES AND FACTS

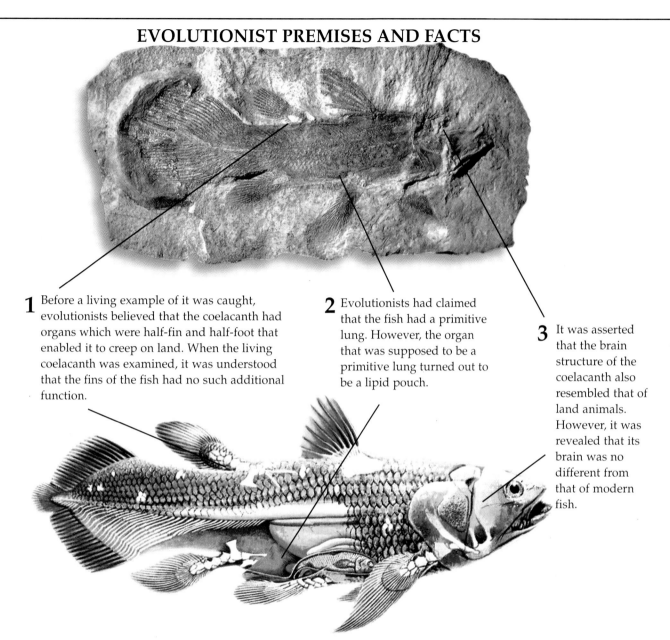

1 Before a living example of it was caught, evolutionists believed that the coelacanth had organs which were half-fin and half-foot that enabled it to creep on land. When the living coelacanth was examined, it was understood that the fins of the fish had no such additional function.

2 Evolutionists had claimed that the fish had a primitive lung. However, the organ that was supposed to be a primitive lung turned out to be a lipid pouch.

3 It was asserted that the brain structure of the coelacanth also resembled that of land animals. However, it was revealed that its brain was no different from that of modern fish.

to be nothing but a lipid pouch.[29] Furthermore, the coelacanth, which was introduced as "a reptile candidate getting prepared to pass from sea to land", was in reality a fish that lived in the depths of the oceans and always stayed more than 180 metres below the surface.[30]

THE DIFFERENCE BETWEEN FINS AND FEET

The reason why evolutionists imagine the coelacanth and similar fish to be "ancestors of land animals" is that these fish have bony fins. They suppose that these bones turned into legs over time. However, there is a basic difference between the bones of these fish and the legs of land-dwelling animals:

The bones of fish are not attached to the spinal column of the animal, as we see in the picture above. In land-dwelling animals, however, bones are directly fastened to the vertebral column, as we see in the picture below. Therefore, the claim that these fins gradually turned into legs is completely groundless.

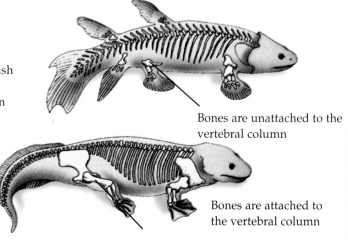

Bones are unattached to the vertebral column

Bones are attached to the vertebral column

Reptiles

The theory of evolution is also unable to account for the origin of reptiles. The members of this specific class have appeared distinctly without undergoing any evolutionary process. The physiological features of reptiles are widely different from those of their alleged ancestors, the amphibians.

Dinosaurs, lizards, turtles and crocodiles… All of these species belong to the living class called "reptiles". Some reptiles, such as dinosaurs, are extinct but some are still alive.

Reptiles have particular features, such as their bodies being covered by plate-like structures called "scales". They are cold-blooded, which means that they cannot generate their own body heat. That is why they need direct sunlight to warm up their bodies. They give birth to their young by laying eggs.

Evolutionists cannot explain how reptiles came into being. The conventional evolutionist allegation on this issue is that reptiles evolved from amphibians. However, there is not a single scrap of evidence to prove this. On the contrary, an examination of amphibians and reptiles demonstrates that there are very great physiological differences between these two living groups and that a half-reptile/half-amphibian has no chances of survival.

Accordingly, such a creature does not exist in the fossil record. Renowned evolutionist paleontologist, Lewis L. Carroll, admits this fact in his article titled "The Problem of the Origin of Reptiles":

> *Unfortunately not a single specimen of an appropriate reptilian ancestor is known prior to the appearance of true reptiles. The absence of such ancestral forms leaves many problems of the amphibian-reptilian transition unanswered.*[31]

THE *SEYMOURIA* MISCONCEPTION
Evolutionists at one time claimed that the *Seymouria* fossil (left) was a transitional form between amphibians and reptiles. According to this scenario, *Seymouria* was "the primitive ancestor of reptiles." However, subsequent fossil discoveries showed that reptiles were living on Earth some 30 million years before *Seymouria*.[32] In the light of this, evolutionists had to relinquish their claims regarding *Seymouria*.

Moreover, there are also insurmountable boundaries between reptile species such as reptiles, dinosaurs or lizards. All of these distinct species arose suddenly and distinctly on the Earth, because God so created them. This fact is thus stated in the Qur'an:

God created every animal from water. Some of them go on their bellies, some of them on two legs, and some on four. God creates whatever He wills. God has power over all things. (Surat an-Nur: 45)

THE END OF DINOSAURS

Dinosaurs were the greatest land-dwelling animals that have ever lived. With their perfectly designed bodies, they lived on Earth for a long time. According to a consensus among scientists, they have become extinct because of a meteor disaster. This phenomenon was divinely planned so as to make the Earth fit for mammals and in particular human beings, which were created subsequently (according to geological records).

TURTLES ARE ALWAYS THE SAME

There is no difference between the ancient fossil reptiles and their counterparts today. The 100 million-year-old sea turtle on the left is exactly the same as its modern counterpart.

THE DIFFERENCE IN THE EGGS

One of the contradictions of the amphibian-reptile evolutionary scenario is the structure of the eggs. Amphibian eggs, which develop in water, have a jelly-like structure and a permeable membrane. Reptile eggs, however, have a solid and water-proof structure adapted to land conditions, as we see in the dinosaur egg reconstruction here. In order for an amphibian to become "reptilian", its eggs must turn into reptile eggs. Yet this is impossible.

Birds and Reptiles

Evolutionists make the claim that birds evolved from reptiles. When we examine the structure of these two living classes, however, we see that this assertion is extremely unscientific.

Evolutionists claim that birds evolved from small-structured, reptilian dinosaurs. A comparison between birds and reptiles, however, demonstrates that these living classes are very different from each other and no evolution whatsoever could have taken place between them. There are many structural differences between birds and reptiles. The most important one is their bone structure. Dinosaurs, the alleged ancestors of birds, according to evolutionists, have thick and solid bones because of their massive structure. Whereas the bones of living and extinct birds are hollow and thus very light. This light-weight bone structure is very important in the flight of birds.

Another important difference between reptiles and birds is their metabolic structure. While reptiles have the slowest metabolic rate in the world of living things, birds hold the highest records in this field. For instance, the body heat of a house sparrow can rise up to 48ºC because of its fast metabolism. On the other hand, reptiles are not even capable of producing their own body heat and instead warm up under the sun. Reptiles are the least energy-consuming animals in nature, whereas birds are the most energy-consuming animals.

THE DISTINCTIVE TRAITS OF REPTILES
In the world of vertebrates, reptiles are one of the groups that least resemble birds. While birds are warm-blooded, reptiles are not even capable of producing their own body heat. With the structure of their skin, their metabolism, and their skeletal system, reptiles are ultimately created to live on land.

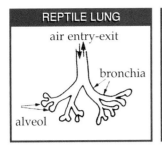

REPTILE LUNG

air entry-exit

bronchia

alveol

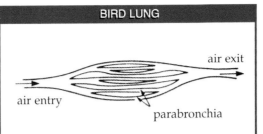

BIRD LUNG

air exit

air entry

parabronchia

Bird lungs function in a completely contrary way to land animal lungs. The latter inhale and exhale through the same air passages. In birds, while the air enters the lung from the front, it goes out from the back. This distinct "design" is specially made for birds, which need great amounts of oxygen during flight. It is impossible for this structure to have evolved from reptile lungs, because respiration would be impossible with an "intermediate" form between these two different lung structures.

THE FUNCTION OF FEATHERS
Unlike reptiles, the bodies of birds are covered with feathers. Responsible for the aerodynamic function in birds, feathers also help them retain their body heat.

The respiratory system of birds also differs greatly from that of reptiles. Reptiles and mammals take air into their lungs through their trachea and then give it back through the same pipe. In birds, however, air makes a one-way journey through the lung channels; it enters from one side and departs from the other. Thanks to this respiratory system that does not exist in any other living class, birds make extremely efficient use of air. This system enables them to fly even at an altitude of 8,000 meters, where oxygen is very scarce.

Another characteristic that raises an unsurpassable barrier between birds and reptiles is feathers, a structure specific to birds. The bodies of reptiles are covered with scales, whereas the bodies of birds are covered with feathers.

Put briefly, numerous differences between birds and reptiles definitively refute the evolutionist claim that reptiles gradually evolved into birds. Birds and reptiles are living classes God created to be quite distinct from each other.

Alan Feduccia, a professor from the University of North Carolina, strongly opposes the theory that birds have a kinship with dinosaurs on the basis of scientific discoveries, despite the fact that he is an evolutionist himself:

> Well, I've studied bird skulls for 25 years and I don't see any similarities whatsoever. I just don't see it... The theropod (a major group of dinosaurs) origins of birds, in my opinion, will be the greatest embarrassment of paleontology of the 20th century.[33]

BIRDS' SPECIAL SKELETAL SYSTEM
Unlike dinosaur and reptile bones, bird bones are hollow. This gives the body stability and lightness. Birds' skeletal structure is employed in designing aeroplanes, bridges and other structures in our own time.

FEDUCCIA'S DENIAL
Famous ornithologist Alan Feduccia thinks that the theory of the evolution of birds from reptiles is simply nonsense.

Archaeopteryx Misconception

A reconstruction
of *Archaeopteryx*

Evolutionists point to the Archaeopteryx fossil as the only evidence to support their claim that "birds evolved from dinosaurs". The latest discoveries, however, prove that this creature is simply an extinct bird species.

The most important intermediate form candidate that evolutionists refer to is a 150 million-year-old fossil bird called *Archaeopteryx*. Evolutionists claim that this fossil bird was a semi-dinosaur which could not fly properly.

This evolutionist claim proven false over and over again, collapsed for good with an *Archaeopteryx* fossil unearthed in 1992.

The absence of a "sternum", that is the chest bone, in this creature, which is essential for flight muscles, was held up as the most important evidence that this bird could not fly properly. The seventh *Archaeopteryx* fossil unearthed in 1992 revealed that the chest bone that evolutionists have long assumed to be missing actually existed. The presence of this bone proved that *Archaeopteryx* was a flying bird. [34]

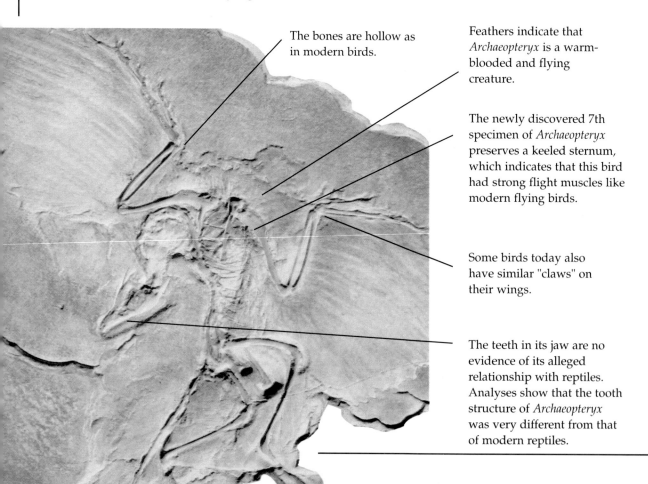

The bones are hollow as in modern birds.

Feathers indicate that *Archaeopteryx* is a warm-blooded and flying creature.

The newly discovered 7th specimen of *Archaeopteryx* preserves a keeled sternum, which indicates that this bird had strong flight muscles like modern flying birds.

Some birds today also have similar "claws" on their wings.

The teeth in its jaw are no evidence of its alleged relationship with reptiles. Analyses show that the tooth structure of *Archaeopteryx* was very different from that of modern reptiles.

TALES FROM EVOLUTIONISTS

Under the pretence of being scientific, evolutionists often allege that "small dinosaurs took wing and became birds." However, their explanation of how this transformation took place is practically a fairy tale. As these evolutionist sketches illustrate, they say that some dinosaurs who flapped their front legs to hunt flies gradually "took wing". A sheer figment of the imagination, this scenario brings along an interesting question with it: How then did flies, which were not only already flying but also displaying an aerodynamic wonder by fluttering their wings 500 times a second synchronously, take wing?

In addition, it has been proved that two other points which evolutionists mention while presenting *Archaeopteryx* as an intermediate form – the claws on its wings and the teeth in its mouth – do not in any way imply that this bird is an intermediate form. It has been observed that two bird species living today, touraco and hoatzin both have claws on their wings by which to hold on to branches. Also, there have been different bird species throughout history that had teeth. Moreover, according to the measurements of famous ornithologists, such as Martin, Stewart and Whetstone, the tooth structure of *Archaeopteryx* was completely different from that of reptiles.[35] All these findings show that the evolutionary claims that *Archaeopteryx* is an intermediate form have no scientific basis.

ASYMMETRIC FEATHERS

The feathers of all modern flying birds are asymmetric. This form gives an aerodynamic function to birds. The fact that *Archaeopteryx*'s feathers were also asymmetric invalidates the evolutionary claim that this bird could not fly.

Confuciusornis fossil and an illustration of the bird

OTHER TOOTHLESS BEAKS

Confuciusornis, whose fossil is seen here, lived in the same geological period as *Archaeopteryx*. Unlike *Archaeopteryx*, however, it had no teeth in its beak. This discovery revealed that *Archaeopteryx* was not "primitive", but was an original bird species.

Hoatzin

HOATZIN'S CLAWS

Some bird species living today have features similar to those of *Archaeopteryx*. For instance, the hoatzin bird also has claw-like structures on its wings.

Bird Feathers

Feathers, which have an extremely complex design and aerodynamic characteristics, are unique to birds. The claim that bird feathers evolved from reptile scales is completely groundless.

The bodies of reptiles are covered with scales, whereas the bodies of birds are covered with feathers. Since evolutionists consider reptiles the ancestors of birds, they are obliged to claim that bird feathers have evolved from reptile scales. However, there is no similarity between scales and feathers.

A professor of physiology and neurobiology from the University of Connecticut, A.H. Brush, accepts this reality, although he is an evolutionist: "Every feature from gene structure and organization, to development, morphogenesis and tissue organization is different (in feathers and scales)."[36] Moreover, Prof. Brush examines the protein structure of bird feathers and argues that it is "unique among vertebrates."[37]

There is no fossil evidence to prove that bird feathers evolved from reptile scales. On the contrary, "feathers appear suddenly in the fossil record, as an 'undeniably unique' character distinguishing birds" as Prof. Brush states.[38] Besides, in reptiles, no epidermal structure has yet been detected that provides an origin for bird feathers.[39]

FEATHERS AND SCALES
The theory of evolution is compelled to propose that feathers that are perfectly designed for flight evolved from reptile scales. Feathers and scales, however, are completely different from each other in terms of genetic origins and embryologic development. Above is the detailed structure of a bird feather and on the side are the scales of a reptile.

The "Feathered dinosaur fossils discovered in China" story, which came to light in 1996 amidst great media propaganda was totally unfounded, and it was realised in 1997 that the *Sinosauropteryx* fossil in question possessed no structures resembling feathers.[40]

On the other hand, when we examine bird feathers closely, we come across a very complex design that cannot be explained by any evolutionary process. The famous ornithologist Alan Feduccia states that "every feature of them has aerodynamic functions. They are extremely light, have the ability to lift up which increases in lower speeds, and may return to their previous position very easily". Then he continues, "I cannot really understand how an organ perfectly designed for flight may have emerged for another need at the beginning".[41]

The design of feathers also compelled Charles Darwin to ponder over them. Moreover, the perfect aesthetics of the peafowl's feathers had made him "sick" (his own words). In a letter he wrote to Asa Gray on April 3, 1860, he said "I remember well the time when the thought of the eye made me cold all over, but I have got over this stage of complaint..." And then continued: "... and now trifling particulars of structure often make me very uncomfortable. The sight of a feather in a peacock's tail, whenever I gaze at it, makes me sick!"[42]

THE PEACOCK AND DARWIN
The feathers of peacocks are a very explicit example of design. They make a human being think in what a beautiful and perfect form God created living things. However, Darwin became "sick" every time he saw this beauty.

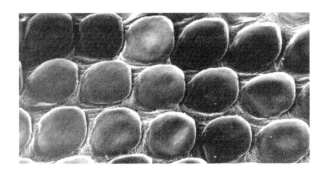

Close-up of reptile scales. As we see clearly, scales are overlapping hard skin parts. They have no resemblance whatsoever to feathers.

STRUCTURE OF FEATHERS
Bird feathers develop on either side of hollow shafts that are directly fastened on to the animal's skeletal bones. This structure is completely different from the scales of reptiles, the so-called ancestors of birds. Scales have nothing to do with skeletal bones.

The Origin of Mammals

Contrary to evolutionist claims, mammals emerged on Earth suddenly without any predecessors. Moreover, evolutionists have no explanation for the origin of distinct mammal groups.

As so far examined, the theory of evolution proposes that some imaginary creatures that came out of the sea transformed themselves into reptiles and that birds were formed by the evolution as that of reptiles. According to the same scenario, reptiles are the ancestors not only of birds but also of mammals. However, on the one hand, there are big, structural gaps between reptiles, which have scales on their bodies, which are cold-blooded, and which reproduce by laying eggs, and on the other, mammals, which have fur on their bodies, which are warm-blooded, and which reproduce by giving birth to live offspring.

An example of the structural barriers between reptiles and mammals is their jaw structure. Mammals' mandibles consist of only one mandibular bone and the teeth are placed on this bone. In reptiles, however, there are three little bones on both sides of the mandible.

Another basic difference is that all mammals have three bones in their middle ear (hammer, anvil, and stirrup). In all reptiles, there is a single bone in the middle ear. Evolutionists claim that the reptile jaw and reptile middle ear evolved gradually into the mammal jaw and ear. Yet the question of how this change occurred remains unanswered. In particular, the question of how an ear with a single bone evolved into an ear with three bones and how the process of hearing kept on functioning in the meanwhile can never be explained.

SEA MAMMALS AND BEARS
Sea mammals, such as dolphins and whales, are the primary animals that put evolutionists into a quandary. According to evolution, these animals ought to have evolved from land mammals, but there is no land animal that can be considered the "ancestor" of these species. In his book *The Origin of Species*, Darwin asserted that "whales had evolved from bears that tried to swim." Later, however, he realized the unreasonableness of this claim and omitted this subject from the latest edition of his book.

THE FOSSIL EVIDENCE

There is no difference between mammal fossils dozens of millions of years old and the mammals living today. Furthermore, these fossils emerge suddenly, with no connection to any species that had gone before.

THE PROBLEM OF FURS

The bodies of mammals are covered by furs or hairs, which is a characteristic that is not found in any other living group. The bodies of reptiles, the alleged ancestors of mammals, however, are covered with scales. Evolutionists prefer to keep silent in response to the question of how scales have been transformed into mammal furs.

Not surprisingly, not a single fossil to link reptiles and mammals is to be found. This is why evolutionist paleontologist Roger Lewin was forced to say that "the transition to the first mammal... is still an enigma".[43]

George Gaylord Simpson, one of the biggest evolutionary authorities in the 20th century makes the following comment on this fact that is quite perplexing for evolutionists:

> *The most puzzling event in the history of life on earth is the change from the Mesozoic, the Age of Reptile, to the Age of Mammals. It is as if the curtain were rung down suddenly on the stage where all the leading roles were taken by reptiles, especially dinosaurs, in great numbers and bewildering variety, and rose again immediately to reveal the same setting but an entirely new cast, a cast in which the dinosaurs do not appear at all, other reptiles are supernumeraries, and all the leading parts are played by mammals of sorts barely hinted at in the preceding acts.*[44]

All of these demonstrate that mammals also appeared on Earth suddenly and fully formed, without any ancestors. This is concrete evidence of the fact that they were created by God.

BATS AND THE SONAR SYTEM

Bats, the only flying mammal species, are one of the organisms that challenge evolution. Evolutionists assert that bats evolved step by step, but they have no consistent answer about the origin of their wings. Moreover, bat fossils aged 50 million years demonstrate that these animals came into being in their present state.

Moreover, bats have a very sensitive sonar system. With their large ears, they sense and analyze the echo of the high-pitched sounds they emit. The emergence of such a complex system cannot be attributed to chance.

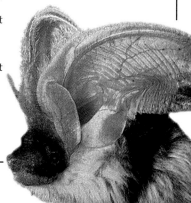

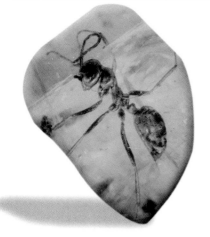

Living Fossils

There is no difference between fossil life forms dating back hundreds of millions of years and their counterparts living today. This fact utterly disproves the evolutionary claim.

Ant fossil preserved in amber, some 100 million years old. No different from the ants in our day.

The theory of evolution argues that living things are in constant change, continuously developing through coincidences. The fossil record, however, indicates just the opposite. When we look at fossils, we see that there is no difference between life forms that lived hundreds of millions of years ago and their counterparts living today. Modern fish, reptiles and mammals are exactly the same as the fish, reptiles and mammals that appeared for the first time on the Earth. Some living species are driven to extinction, but no species has turned into another species. This makes it clear that all living species were created by God to be quite distinct from each other, and they have not undergone any evolution since the day they were created.

BEE FOSSIL
Petrified bee fossil aged 60 million years; no different from the bees in our day.

NO CHANGE IN STRUCTURE FOR 300 MILLION YEARS
Called *Triops Cancriformis* in scientific literature, this shrimp-like creature has not undergone any change for 300 million years.

DRAGON-FLY AND ITS FOSSIL
There is no difference between this 150 million-year-old dragon-fly fossil and the living dragon-fly.

FISH

The fish fossil dating back 200 million years (below) shows that ancient fish and their modern counterparts are not different from each other.

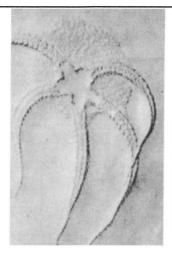

STARFISH

A 400 million-year-old starfish fossil and a living starfish

NAUTILUS IS ALWAYS THE SAME

The invertebrate species called *Nautilus*, which proliferates in the seas of today, is also found in abundance in fossil form in the Cambrian strata dating back 520 million years. Since the day of its creation, the *Nautilus* has not undergone any evolution.

MAY BUG UNCHANGED

The living specimen of the may bug of the *baetidae* class and its 220 million-year-old fossil stored in amber. A comparison of the two shows that this bug has not undergone any evolution throughout the ages.

PLANTS ARE ALSO THE SAME

"The evolution of plants" is also nothing but a tale. On the side, you see a living specimen of a plant species called acer monspessulanum and its 30 million-year-old fossil.

The Tale of Man's Evolution

Just like evolutionists' other claims on the origin of life forms, their claim about the origin of man has likewise no scientific basis. Discoveries show that "the evolution of man" is simply a tale.

Darwin put forward his claim that human beings and monkeys descended from a common ancestor in his book *The Descent of Man* published in 1871. From that time onwards, the followers of Darwin have tried to bolster this claim. But despite all the research that has been carried out, the claim of "human evolution" has not been backed up by any concrete scientific discovery, particularly in the fossil field.

The man in the street is for the most part unaware of this fact, and thinks that the claim of human evolution is supported by a great deal of firm evidence. The reason for this incorrect opinion is that the subject is frequently discussed in the media and presented as a proven fact. But real experts on the subject are aware that the claim of "human evolution" has no scientific foundation. David Pilbeam, one of Harvard University's palaeontologists, says the following:

> *If you brought in a smart scientist from another discipline and showed him the meagre evidence we've got he'd surely say, 'forget it: there isn't enough to go on.'*[45]

And William Fix, the author of an important book on the subject of palaeoanthropology, makes this comment:

> *There are numerous scientists and popularizers today who have the temerity to tell us that there is 'no doubt' how man originated. If only they had the evidence.*[46]

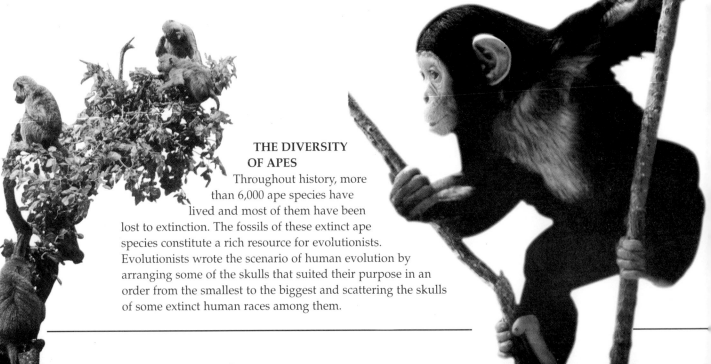

THE DIVERSITY OF APES
Throughout history, more than 6,000 ape species have lived and most of them have been lost to extinction. The fossils of these extinct ape species constitute a rich resource for evolutionists. Evolutionists wrote the scenario of human evolution by arranging some of the skulls that suited their purpose in an order from the smallest to the biggest and scattering the skulls of some extinct human races among them.

This claim of evolution, which "lacks any evidence," starts the human family tree with a species of monkey called *Australopithecus*. According to the claim, *Australopithecus* began to walk upright over time, his brain grew, and passed through a series of stages to come to man's present state (*Homo sapiens.*) But the fossil record does not back up this scenario. Despite the claim of all kinds of intermediate forms, there is an impassable barrier between the fossil remains respectively of man and monkeys. Furthermore, it has been revealed that the species which are portrayed as each others' ancestors are actually contemporary species that lived in the same period. Ernst Mayr, one of the most important proponents of the theory of evolution in the 20th century, accepts this truth: "The chain reaching as far as *Homo sapiens* is actually lost."[47]

Ernst Mayr, one of the founders of neo-Darwinism, admits that the scenario of "man's evolution" has found no evidence in the fossil record.

THE FOSSIL RECORD DISPROVES EVOLUTION
The scenario of "human evolution" has no basis in the fossil record just as evolutionists' other scenarios about living species. Contrary to the propaganda spread by the media, there is no fossil evidence demonstrating that men and apes come from a common ancestor.

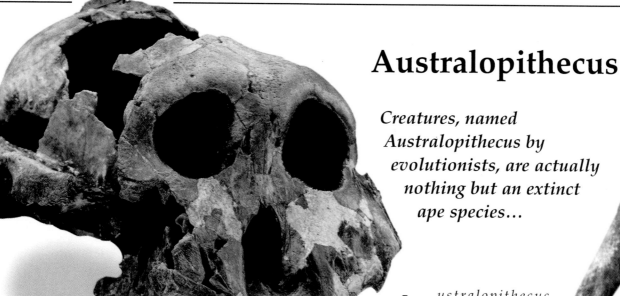

Australopithecus

Creatures, named Australopithecus by evolutionists, are actually nothing but an extinct ape species...

A skull fossil of *Australopithecus bosei* species coded as OH-5

Australopithecus means "southern ape". Falling into different categories, all *Australopithecus* species are extinct apes that resemble the apes of today. Their cranial capacities are the same, or smaller than the chimpanzees of our day. There are projecting parts in their hands and feet which they used to climb trees, just like today's chimpanzees, and their feet have grasping abilities to hold on to the branches. Many characteristics such as the closeness of the eyes, sharp molar teeth, mandibular structure, long arms, short legs, are evidence of these creatures being no different from today's apes.

Evolutionists claim that although the *Australopithecus* species have the anatomy of an ape, they walked upright like humans.

Extensive research done on various *Australopithecus* specimens by two world-renowned anatomists from England and the USA, namely, Lord Solly Zuckerman and Prof. Charles Oxnard, has shown that these creatures were not bipedal and had the same sort of movement as today's apes. Having studied the bones of these fossils for a period of 15 years, with funding from the British government, Lord Zuckerman and his team of 5 specialists reached the conclusion – although Zuckerman was an

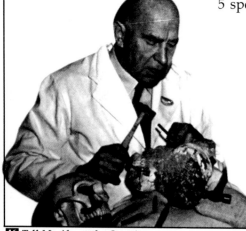

DART AND HIS CHILD
The first *Australopithecus* fossil was discovered by evolutionist palaeontologist Raymond Dart. The first specimen discovered by Dart was named the "Taung Child". Dart had suggested that this fossil, which belonged to a very young individual, had "human-like" features. Discoveries that were made in the following years, however, showed that the *Australopithecus* species definitely had an ape's face.

Science&Vie
Le plaisir de savoir

ORIGINES DE L'HOMME
Adieu Lucy
Les découvertes qui bouleversent notre généalogie

Astronautique
Bientôt un cosmonaute

Encyclopédie
XXI° siècle
La révolution quantique

Effet de serre
Les vraies conséquences pour la France

"FAREWELL LUCY!"
Scientific findings countered the evolutionist propositions on "Lucy", the most famous specimen of the *Australopithecus* species. The well-known French science journal, *Science et Vie*, admitted this fact in its February 1999 issue with the headline "Farewell Lucy" (Adieu Lucy) and the statement that *Australopithecus* could not be considered the ancestor of man.

evolutionist himself – that Australopithecines were only an ordinary ape species and were definitely not bipedal.[48] Correspondingly, Oxnard, who is also an evolutionist, also likened the skeletal structure of *Australopithecus* to that of modern orang-utans.[49]

The detailed analyses conducted by the American anthropologist Holly Smith in 1994 on the teeth of *Australopithecus* indicated that *Australopithecus* was an ape species.[50]

Within the same year, Fred Spoor, Bernard Wood and Frans Zonneveld, all specialists on anatomy, reached the same conclusion through a totally different method. This method was based on the comparative analysis of the semi-circular canals in the inner ear of humans and apes which provided for sustaining balance. The inner ear canals of all *Australopithecus* specimens analysed by Spoor, Wood and Zonneveld were the same as those of modern apes.[51] This finding once more showed that the *Australopithecus* species is a species similar to modern apes.

***AUSTRALOPITHECUS* AND CHIMPANZEE**
The skull of the *Australopithecus aferensis* and that of the modern chimpanzee are very similar to each other. This similarity verifies that creatures falling into the *Australopithecus* classification are an ape species that have nothing to do with humans.

IMAGINARY DRAWINGS
Such evolutionary drawings depicting *Australopithecus* walking have been disproved by the latest scientific discoveries.

Skull coded as A.L. 444-2 that belongs to the *Australopithecus afarensis* species

Chimpanzee skull

Homo Erectus

Presented as "primitive man" by evolutionists, Homo Erectus is actually a lost human race. The differences between Homo Erectus and us are simply racial differences.

A skull dating back some 13,000 years unearthed in Kow Swamp in Australia that has the characteristics of both modern man and *Homo erectus*.

A typical *Homo erectus* skull found in Koobi Fora in Africa in 1975.

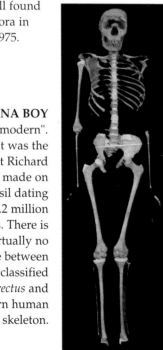

TURKANA BOY
"Tall and modern". That was the comment Richard Leakey made on this fossil dating back 2.2 million years. There is virtually no difference between this fossil classified as *Homo erectus* and the modern human skeleton.

In the scheme of "man's evolution" devised by evolutionists, fossils classified as *Homo erectus* come after the *Australopithecus* species. (The classification, "*Homo habilis*", which was proposed by certain evolutionists, has been included in the *Australopithecus* species in recent years.)

As the word "erect" implies, "*Homo erectus*" means a "man walking upright". Evolutionists have had to separate these men from previous ones by adding the quality of "erectness", because all the available *Homo erectus* fossils are straight to an extent not observed in any of the *Australopithecus* or *Homo habilis* specimens. There is no difference between the skeleton of modern man and that of *Homo erectus*.

A good indication of this is the "Turkana Boy" fossil that is included in the *Homo erectus* class. It is confirmed that the fossil was of a 12-year-old boy, who would have been 1.83 meters tall in his adolescence. The upright skeleton structure of the fossil is no different from that of modern man, on which point American paleoanthropologist Alan Walker said that he doubted that "the average pathologist could tell the difference between the fossil skeleton and that of a modern human."[52]

The primary reason for evolutionists to define *Homo erectus* as "primitive" is the cranial capacity of its skull (900-1100 cc), which is smaller than that of the average modern man, and its thick eyebrow projections. However, there are many people living today in the world who have the same cranial capacity as *Homo erectus* (for instance the pygmies) and there are some other races that have protruding eyebrows (for instance the Australian Aborigines).

It is a commonly agreed fact that differences in cranial capacity do not necessarily denote differences in intelligence or abilities. Intelligence depends on the internal organisation of the brain rather than its volume.[53]

Even evolutionist Richard Leakey states that the differences

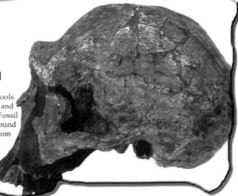

Ancient mariners

Early humans were much smarter than we suspected

OUR ancestors made organised sea journeys more than 700 000 years earlier than previously thought—and they probably used language to coordinate their efforts.

This surprising new theory comes from palaeoanthropologist Mike Morwood and his colleagues at the University of New England in northern New South Wales. It is the result of an intriguing find during their exploration of an ancient lake bed at Mata Menge on the Island of Fl...

ash surrounding the tools were between 800 000 and 880 000 years old. Fossil plants and animals found near the tools dated from the same period.

The researchers believe the tools were used by the ancestral human species *Homo*

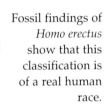

MARINE ENGINEER *HOMO ERECTUS*

News published in *New Scientist* on March 14th, 1998, tells us that the humans called *Homo Erectus* by evolutionists were practicing seamanship 700,000 years ago. These humans, who had enough knowledge and technology to build a vessel and possess a culture that made use of sea transport, can hardly be called primitive.

Fossil findings of *Homo erectus* show that this classification is of a real human race.

between *Homo erectus* and modern man are no more than racial variance: *"One would also see differences in the shape of the skull, in the degree of protrusion of the face, the robustness of the brows and so on. These differences are probably no more pronounced than we see today between the separate geographical races of modern humans."*[54]

In short, human beings, whom evolutionists classify as *Homo erectus*, are a lost human race whose level of intelligence is no different from our own. There is, on the other hand, a huge gap between *Homo erectus*, a human race, and the apes that preceded it in the "human evolution" scenario, (*Australopithecus*, or *Homo habilis*). This means that the first men appeared in the fossil record suddenly and right away without any evolutionary history. There can be no clearer indication of their being created.

MODERN *HOMO ERECTUS*

In its 23 December 1996 issue, *Time* magazine covered a 27,000-year-old *Homo erectus* found on the Island of Java. The fact that *Homo erectus* existed till very recent times is evidence that it is not a different species but a modern human race.

AUSTRALIAN NATIVE PEOPLE

Aborigines, the native people of Australia, who are still living today, have great similarities to *Homo erectus* in terms of their cranial features.

A Lost Human Race: Neanderthals

If we had seen a Neanderthal in the street today, we would think him or her to be no different from other people.

Today, it has been definitively verified that Neanderthal man, who is presented as the "primitive ancestor of man" by evolutionists, is simply a lost human race.

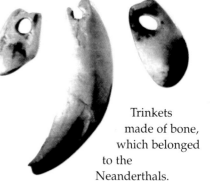

Trinkets made of bone, which belonged to the Neanderthals.

Neanderthals are human beings who suddenly appeared 100,000 years ago in Europe and disappeared–or were assimilated by being blended with other races–quietly yet quickly 35,000 years ago. Their only difference from modern man is their skeleton being more robust and their cranial capacity slightly bigger.

Neanderthals are a human race and this fact is admitted by almost everybody today. Evolutionists have tried very hard to present them as "a primitive species", yet all findings indicate that they were no different from a "robust" man walking on the street today. A prominent authority on the subject, Erik Trinkaus, a paleoanthropologist from New Mexico University writes:

> *Detailed comparisons of Neanderthal skeletal remains with those of modern humans have shown that there is nothing in Neanderthal anatomy that conclusively indicates locomotor, manipulative, intellectual, or linguistic abilities inferior to those of modern humans.*[55]

FALSE NEANDERTHAL MASKS FROM EVOLUTIONISTS

Evolutionists expended great effort on presenting the Neanderthal race as primitive cave men. Imaginary pictures, such as the one we see here, took their place in textbooks. However, today, evolutionists have also had to admit that Neanderthal man had an advanced culture.

Neanderthal man had thick eyebrow projections just like those of the Australian natives living today.

The cranial capacity of Neanderthals was bigger than that of modern man by 150 cc. This finding refuted the evolutionist claim that "the brain got bigger over time."

The skull of Neanderthal man differed slightly from that of modern man.

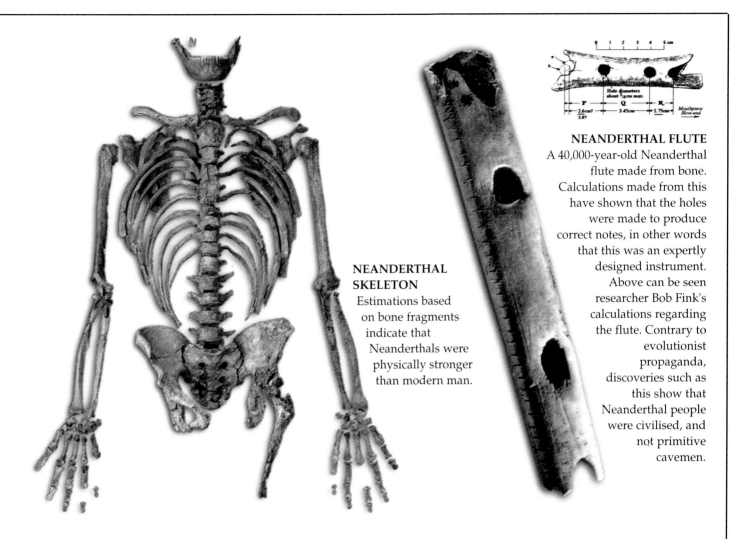

NEANDERTHAL SKELETON

Estimations based on bone fragments indicate that Neanderthals were physically stronger than modern man.

NEANDERTHAL FLUTE

A 40,000-year-old Neanderthal flute made from bone. Calculations made from this have shown that the holes were made to produce correct notes, in other words that this was an expertly designed instrument. Above can be seen researcher Bob Fink's calculations regarding the flute. Contrary to evolutionist propaganda, discoveries such as this show that Neanderthal people were civilised, and not primitive cavemen.

Many contemporary researchers define Neanderthal man as a sub-species of modern man and call him "*Homo sapiens neandertalensis*". The findings testify that Neanderthals buried their dead, fashioned musical instruments, and had cultural affinities with the *Homo sapiens sapiens* living during the same period. To put it precisely, Neanderthals are a "robust" human race that simply disappeared in time.

THE NEANDERTHALS' SEWING NEEDLE

Another pieces of fossil evidence giving us an idea of the civilization of Neanderthals is the sewing needle seen above. This needle, which is estimated to date back 26,000 years, shows that the Neanderthals also had the ability to make clothing.

NEANDERTHALS AND ESKIMOS

A comparison made between Neanderthal man and modern human races. To the far left and second from left are Neanderthal men. Neanderthals bear the greatest resemblance to Eskimos who live in cold climates today.

The Collapse of the Family Tree

The scenario of "man's family tree" is refuted by fossil evidence. It is understood today that species which are presented as ancestors of one another are actually different races that lived at the same period.

The so-called "evolutionary tree" made by evolutionist biologist Ernst Haeckel at the close of the 19th century.

The scenario of "human evolution" is a totally fiction. In order for such a family tree to exist, a gradual evolution from ape to man should have taken place and the fossil record of this process should have been found. However, there is a huge gap between apes and humans. Skeletal structures, cranial capacities, and other such criteria as walking upright or bent sharply forward are what distinguish humans from apes.

Another significant finding proving that there can be no family tree among these different species is that the species that are presented as ancestors of each other in fact lived concurrently. If, as the evolutionists claim, australopithecines converted to *Homo habilis* and if they, in turn, converted to *Homo erectus*, the eras they lived in should necessarily have followed each other. However, there is no such chronological order. The evolutionist paleontologist Alan Walker confirms this fact by stating that "there is evidence from East Africa for late-surviving small *Australopithecus* individuals that were contemporaneous first with H. Habilis, then with H. erectus."[56] Louis Leakey has found fossils of *Australopithecus*, *Homo habilis* and *Homo erectus* almost next to each other in Olduvai Gorge region, Bed II layer.[57]

THE FAMILY TREE EXISTS ONLY IN DRAWINGS
The schemes of "the family tree of man", products of the wide imaginative power of evolutionists, are disproved by the fossil record.

The family tree concept that stretches from the primates to apes, and then over to man, exists only in the dreams of evolutionists.

A paleontologist from Harvard University, Stephen Jay Gould, explains this deadlock of evolution although he is an evolutionist himself:

"What has become of our ladder if there are three coexisting lineages of hominids (A. africanus, the robust australopithecines, and H. habilis), none clearly derived from another? Moreover, none of the three display any evolutionary trends during their tenure on earth."[58]

When we move on from *Homo erectus* to *Homo sapiens*, we again see that there is no family tree to talk about. There is evidence showing that *Homo erectus* and archaic *Homo sapiens* continued living up to 27,000 years and even 10,000 years before our time. In the Kow swamp in Australia, some 13,000-year-old *Homo erectus* skulls have been found. On Java Island, a *Homo erectus* skull was found that was 27,000 years old.[59]

These finds indicate that the creatures presented as the "ancestors of man" by the theory of evolution are either extinct species that have nothing to do with one another or lost human races.

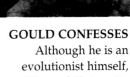

GOULD CONFESSES
Although he is an evolutionist himself, Harvard University Palaeontologist Stephen Jay Gould admits that the scenario of the "human's family tree" has collapsed.

The Bipedalism Impasse

Human beings move in a completely different way from other creatures. No other animal can walk upright on its two feet as humans do. Evolutionists, however, claim that the bipedal upright stride of humans evolved by steps from the apes' quadripedal bent stride.

This claim is not true. Firstly, the fossil record shows that no life form ever had a way of movement in between the human and the ape stride. Detailed examinations of the fossil record prove that creatures of the *Australopithecus* and *Homo habilis* classes walked on all fours and by leaning forward, while human races such as *Homo erectus* and Neanderthal man walked upright just like us. This means that the bipedal upright stride emerged with humans for the first time and all of a sudden.

Besides, anatomical research conducted in recent years establishes that the gradual evolution of the ape stride into the human stride is impossible. In 1996, the British anatomist Robin Crompton, who conducted research into the bipedal stride of humans, concluded that a motion in between the ape stride and the human

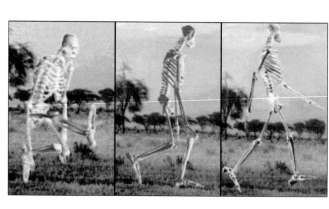

The entire skeletal structure of apes is designed according to the quadripedal stride. Their arms are long and their skeleton is bent forward. Moreover, their hands and feet are curved to enable them to climb trees.

COMPUTER SIMULATIONS
Evolutionists state that the so-called ancestors of man had a "half-bent, half-erect" posture. Computer simulation studies by Robin Crompton demonstrated that such a form of movement is not possible. A living thing must walk either fully upright or fully bent to make the maximum use of energy.

INNER EAR ANALYSIS RESULTS

In the human inner ear, and that of other creatures with complicated structures, there is an organ called the "cochlea," which works out the position of the body relative to the ground. The working of this organ is the same as the implement called a "gyroscope" which maintains the balance of an aeroplane. In order to find out whether the living creatures which were portrayed as man's ancestors walked upright on two legs or not, Spoor carried out studies on this organ, the cochlea. The result he arrived at was that some life forms presented as the ancestor of man had a bent posture just like modern apes and some had an upright posture just like modern humans. This result totally disproves the theory that bipedalism gradually evolved from quadripedalism.

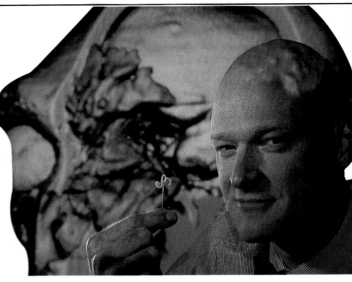

Fred Spoor

stride is not possible. Crompton showed that a living thing can either walk upright or on all fours. A type of in-between stride would be quite ineffective.[60]

The immense gap between man and ape is not limited solely to bipedalism. Many other issues still remain unexplained such as brain capacity, the ability to talk, and so on. Elaine Morgan, an evolutionist paleoanthropologist, makes the following confession in relation to this issue:

Four of the most outstanding mysteries about humans are: 1) why do they walk on two legs? 2) why have they lost their fur? 3) why have they developed such large brains? 4) why did they learn to speak?

The orthodox answers to these questions are: 1) 'We do not yet know'; 2) 'We do not yet know'; 3) 'We do not yet know'; 4) 'We do not yet know'. The list of questions could be considerably lengthened without affecting the monotony of the answers.[61]

In short, "the evolution of man" is nothing but an unsubstantiated tale. Man is created by God already equipped with all the abilities and features he possesses.

IMAGINARY CREATURES

The "half bent" creatures pictured by evolutionists are actually nothing but figments of the imagination. Scientific findings demonstrate that no creatures having a stride in between that of the ape and man ever existed in history.

False Faces

Even if evolutionists are unsuccessful in finding scientific evidence to shore up their theories, they are very successful at one thing: propaganda. The most important elements of this propaganda are the false drawings and designs known as "reconstructions."

Reconstruction can be explained as drawing a picture or constructing a model of a living thing based on a single bone that has been unearthed. The "ape-men" we see in newspapers, magazines, or films are all reconstructions.

The important thing here is how scientific these drawings are. Since fossils are usually disordered and incomplete, any conjecture based on them is likely to be totally imaginative. As a matter of fact, the reconstructions made by evolutionists based on the fossil remains are prepared precisely to suit the purposes of the evolutionary thesis.

At this point, we have to highlight a particular point: studies based on bone remains cannot reveal the "soft tissues" of a creature. The hair, skin, nose, ears, lips, or other facial features of a living thing cannot be determined from its bone remains. It is very easy for someone committed to evolution to devise an imaginary creature by shaping these soft tissues as he wishes.

Earnest A. Hooton from Harvard University, explains the situation like this:

The sketches of evolutionists depict imaginary creatures even in their social setting. Based on no evidence, these illustrations are nothing but propaganda tools.

THE THREE FACES OF ZINJANTHROPUS

Evolutionists go so far in imaginary drawings that they even ascribe different faces to the same skull. The three different reconstructed drawings made for the fossil named *Australopithecus robustus* (Zinjanthropus) is an example of this.

Another famous example of the imagination of evolutionists was the "Nebraska Man" scandal. This was cooked up in 1922 on the basis of a single molar tooth found in Nebraska, USA. With nothing to go on but this single tooth, evolutionists published imaginary drawings of the Nebraska Man and his "wife". It was revealed in 1929 that the tooth in fact belonged to a wild pig.

N. Parker's drawing
National Geographic, September 1960

Maurice Wilson's drawing

Appeared in Sunday Times
April 5, 1964

To attempt to restore the soft parts is an even more hazardous undertaking. The lips, the eyes, the ears, and the nasal tip leave no clues on the underlying bony parts. You can with equal facility model on a Neanderthaloid skull the features of a chimpanzee or the lineaments of a philosopher. These alleged restorations of ancient types of man have very little if any scientific value and are likely only to mislead the public... So put not your trust in reconstructions.[62]

Evolutionists animate the creatures that exist only in their imagination by using the method of "reconstruction" and present them to people as if they are "their ancestors". When they are unable to find the "half-man half-ape" creatures in the fossil record, they prefer to deceive the public with false drawings.

BE CAREFUL WITH THE SOFT TISSUES!

Soft tissues like the eye, nose, ear, skin, hair leave no clues in the fossil record. Yet evolutionists shape these tissues as they wish in the reconstructions they fabricate in their workshops and produce "half-ape half-man" creatures as we see here.

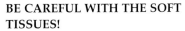

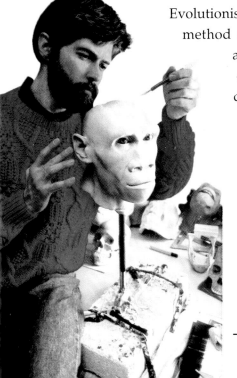

Piltdown Scandal

The Piltdown Man skull was presented to the world over a period of 40 years as the biggest piece of evidence for the claim of "human evolution". This skull, however, was actually the biggest science fraud in history.

The bust of the Piltdown Man which was once displayed in museums.

A well-known doctor and also an amateur paleoanthropologist, Charles Dawson came out with an assertion that he had found a jawbone and a cranial fragment in a pit in Piltdown, England in 1912. Even though the jawbone was more ape-like, the teeth and the skull were like a man's. These specimens were labelled the "Piltdown Man". Alleged to be 500,000 years old, they were displayed as an absolute proof of human evolution in several museums. For more than 40 years, many scientific articles were written on the "Piltdown Man", many interpretations and sketches were made, and the fossil was presented as an important piece of evidence of human evolution. No less than five hundred doctoral theses were written on the subject.[63]

In 1949, Kenneth Oakley from the British Museum's paleontology department attempted to try the method of "fluorine testing", a new test used for determining the date of some old fossils. A trial was carried out on the fossil of the Piltdown Man. The result was astounding. During the test, it was realised that the

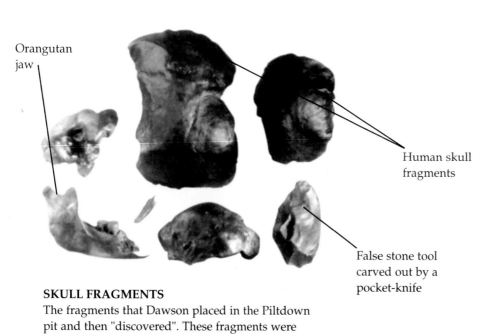

Orangutan jaw

Human skull fragments

False stone tool carved out by a pocket-knife

SKULL FRAGMENTS
The fragments that Dawson placed in the Piltdown pit and then "discovered". These fragments were deftly put together later on.

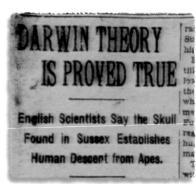

DARWIN THEORY IS PROVED TRUE

English Scientists Say the Skull Found in Sussex Establishes Human Descent from Apes.

THE FANFARE OF EVOLUTIONIST NEWSPAPERS
As soon as Piltdown man was found, many newspapers covered the subject in banner headlines. The above headline was printed in a London newspaper of the time.

jawbone of the Piltdown Man did not contain any fluorine. This indicated that it had remained buried for no more than a few years. The skull, which contained only a small amount of fluorine, showed that it was only a few thousand years old.

Detailed research revealed that Piltdown man was the biggest science fraud in history. This was an artificial skull; the cranium belonged to a 500-year-old man, and the mandibular bone belonged to a recently dead ape! The teeth were thereafter specially arranged in an array and added to the jaw, and the joints were filed in order to resemble that of a man. Then all these pieces were stained with potassium dichromate to give them an ancient appearance.

Le Gros Clark, who was in the team that disclosed the forgery, could not hide his astonishment at this situation and said that "the evidences of artificial abrasion immediately sprang to the eye. Indeed so obvious did they seem it may well be asked - how was it that they had escaped notice before?"[64] In the wake of all this, "Piltdown Man" was hurriedly removed from the British Museum where it had been displayed for more than 40 years.

The Piltdown scandal clearly showed that there was nothing that evolutionists would stop short of doing in order to prove their theories. Moreover, this scandal showed that evolutionists had no findings to reinforce their theories. Since they have no evidence, they prefer to fabricate it themselves.

False fossil Piltdown man was pictured like this in the British press.

Piltdown Man was nothing but a hoax perpetrated by cementing an ape jaw to a human skull.

PROFESSIONAL HOAX
After connecting an orangutan's jaw to the skull, Charles Dawson (left) buried them in a pit. Then the pit was re-opened with Sir Arthur Keith (middle), one of the respectable scientists of the time, in attendance. This was how the Piltdown Man hoax that lasted for 40 years started.

The Piltdown hoax being exposed by the fluorine test.

Why is Evolution Defended?

Since the day of its formulation, the evolutionary theory has served the best interests of materialist philosophy. Today, those who make efforts to keep this theory alive are the proponents of this philosophy.

Why is the theory of evolution still defended despite the obvious evidence against it? The American evolutionist biologist, Michael Walker, makes the following confession as he answers this question:

One is forced to conclude that many scientists and technologists pay lip service to Darwinian theory only because it supposedly excludes a creator.[65]

The only purpose of the promoters of the theory is to foster the materialist philosophy which denies God. Materialism is a blind faith that admits the existence of matter alone and denies all supra-material beings. Since materialists derive their so-called scientific argument from the theory of evolution, they have sustained Darwinism since the day of its inception.

The founder of dialectic materialism (communism), Karl Marx, wrote of Darwin's book, *The Origin of Species*, which laid the basis for the theory of evolution, as "the book which contains the basis in natural history for our view."[66]

Since that day, all materialists, with Marxists in the forefront, blindly defend Darwinism.

Yet, the lie of evolution that has cheated the world for the last 140 years will not live on for long. The British philosopher Malcolm Muggeridge states the inevitable collapse of the theory:

I myself am convinced that the theory of evolution, especially the extent to which it's been applied, will be one of the great jokes in the history books in the future. Posterity will marvel that so very flimsy and dubious an hypothesis could be accepted with the incredible credulity that it has.[67]

TH
LIFE AND LI
CHARLES

Including an Autobi

EDITED B
FRANCIS

IN TWO
V

NE
D. APPLETO

THE CONNECTION WITH MATERIALISM
The materialist philosophy was born in the pagan culture of Ancient Greece. Darwinism laid the so-called scientific foundation for this philosophy, which was revived in the 18th century.

DARWINISM AND RACISM

Another ideology that was nourished by Darwinism was racism. In his book, *The Origin of Species*, Darwin suggested that European white races had progressed in evolution, whereas the other races were still at the same level as apes. These ideas provided a so-called scientific justification for racist thinkers. The racist illustration seen on the side, showing black people and apes in the same tree, is a representation of the impact of Darwinism in 19th century England.

The racist heritage of Darwinism provided the basis for ideologies such as Nazism in the 20th century. The racist views of the Nazi leader Adolf Hitler derived from Darwin's theory of evolution. In Hitler's book *Mein Kampf* (My Struggle), there were views inspired by Darwin's concept of the struggle for existence.

Darwin's Enmity Towards the Turks

The racist views of Charles Darwin were directed against many races among which were the Turks. As quoted from the book titled *The Life and Letters of Charles Darwin* that is composed of Darwin's letters, Darwin referred to the Turkish nation as a "lower race" and then estimated that "lower races will have been eliminated at no very distant date." In the letter Charles Darwin wrote to W. Graham on July 3, 1881, he said: "I could show fight on natural selection having done and doing more for the progress of civilization than you seem inclined to admit. Remember what risk the nations of Europe ran, not so many centuries ago of being overwhelmed by the Turks, and how ridiculous such an idea now is! The more civilized so-called Caucasian races have beaten the Turkish hollow in the struggle for existence. Looking to the world at no very distant date, what an endless number of the lower races will have been eliminated by the higher civilized races throughout the world."[68]

KARL MARX

The first person to understand the importance of Darwin's contribution to materialism was Karl Marx, the founder of communism. Marx showed his sympathy to Darwin by dedicating to him *Das Kapital*, which is considered his greatest work. In the German edition of the book which he sent to Darwin, he wrote: "From a devoted admirer to Charles Darwin"

FRIEDRICH ENGELS

Friedrich Engels, the biggest associate of Marx, regarded the theory of evolution as a great support for materialism. Engels praised Darwin and Marx as being the same: "Just as Darwin discovered the law of evolution in organic nature, so did Marx discover the law of evolution in human history."[69]

The Obvious Truth: Creation

As science demolishes the theory of evolution which seeks to explain forms of life as chance developments, it demonstrates in the process that there is a perfect creation in nature. All living things came into being by God's creation.

The theory of evolution maintains that life is the work of "chance". However, all the scientific evidence we have reviewed in this book shows that this is untrue and life is created with a design too superior to be explained away by chance.

The belief in "chance" was born in the 19th century, when life was supposed to be simple, and it was carried into the 20th century for ideological purposes. Today, however, the scientific community acknowledges how nonsensical this claim is, and a great number of scientists admit that life is the work of a superior Creator. Chandra Wickramasinghe describes the reality he faced as a scientist who had been inculcated into believing in the myth of "chance" for years:

From my earliest training as a scientist, I was very strongly brainwashed to believe that science cannot be consistent with any kind of deliberate creation. That notion has had to be painfully shed. At the moment, I can't find any rational argument to knock down the view which argues for conversion to God. We used to have an open mind; now we realize that the only logical answer to life is creation-and not accidental random shuffling.[70]

One does not need to visit biochemistry laboratories or fossil beds to be able to see this obvious truth. Anyone may see the fact of creation in any part of the world he examines by using his conscience and reason.

FROM A CELL TO A HUMAN BEING

The creation of man in the mother's womb is a miracle on its own. The union of the sperm and the ovum forms a living cell. Then this cell multiplies. The multiplying cells start to differentiate by a secret order. They are arranged and ordered to form bones, eyes, the heart, vessels or the skin. At the end of this intricate process, a single cell turns into a perfect human being. Referring to this creation, God calls out to man:

"O man! What has deluded you in respect of your Noble Lord? He Who created you and formed you and proportioned you and assembled you in whatever way He willed." (Surat al-Infitar: 6-8)

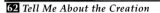

THE CREATION OF THE MOSQUITO

The mosquito has an "ultraviolet vision" system that enables it to locate its prey at night. Its sting, through which it sucks blood, is a complicated tool made up of 6 blades. It is furnished with special secretions that prevent the blood it sucks from coagulating and that are even capable of anesthetizing the human nervous system. With its superior design, even a single mosquito is obvious evidence for creation. God states in the Qur'an:

"God is not ashamed to make an example of a gnat or of an even smaller thing. As for those who believe, they know it is the truth from their Lord." (Surat al-Baqara: 26)

THE CREATION OF THE CAMEL

In the Qur'an, God says **"Have they not looked at the camel - how it was created?"** (Surat al-Gashiyah: 17). When we look at the camel, we see that this animal is specially created for desert conditions. It has a metabolism that enables it to live without water for weeks, it has special tissues to protect its body from the burning sand, and it has even special eyebrow systems that will curtain its eyes against sand storms.

He can easily understand the infinite wisdom, knowledge and power of his Creator by simply thinking how he grew into a human being who is able to read and understand these lines considering that he was just a drop in the beginning.

No one came to this world by chance. God, the Lord of all the worlds, created the entire universe and all of mankind. God describes His creative power in the Qur'an, which He sent down to people as a guide.

Mankind! An example has been made, so listen to it carefully. Those whom you call upon besides God are not even able to create a single fly, even if they were to join together to do it. And if a fly steals something from them, they cannot get it back. How feeble are both the seeker and the sought! They do not measure God with His true measure. God is All-Powerful, Almighty. (Surat al-Hajj: 73-74)

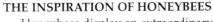

THE INSPIRATION OF HONEYBEES

Honeybees display an extraordinary architectural skill. The hexagonal cells they build are based on complex mathematical calculations. They use a system whereby they can do the maximum storage with the minimum material.

The interesting aspect of the cells is that honeybees start to build the cells from different points and meet in the middle. However, there is no discord at the intersection point. This situation shows that bees are governed from a single centre. God states in the Qur'an that bees act upon His inspiration:

"Your Lord inspired the bees: 'Build dwellings in the mountains and the trees, and also in the structures which men erect. Then eat from every kind of fruit and travel the paths of your Lord, made easy for you to follow.' From their bellies comes a drink of varying colours, containing healing for mankind. There is certainly a sign in that for people who reflect." (Surat an-Nahl: 68-69)

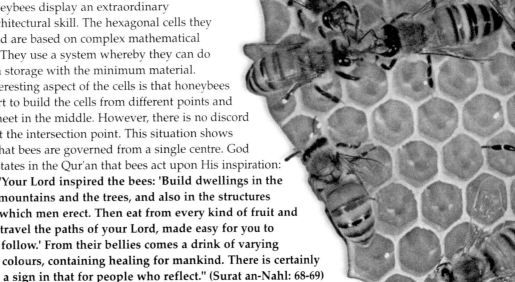

Notes

1) Charles Darwin, The Origin of Species: A Facsimile of the First Edition, Harvard University Press, 1964, p. 184

2) Sidney Fox, Klaus Dose. Molecular Evolution and The Origin of Life. New York: Marcel Dekker, 1977, p. 2

3) Jeffrey Bada, "Origins", Earth, February 1998, p. 40

4) Leslie E. Orgel, "The Origin of Life on Earth", Scientific American, Vol 271, October 1994, p. 78

5) Please see Harun Yahya, The Evolution Deceit, Ta Ha Publishers, 1999, p. 93

6) W.R. Bird, The Origin of Species Revisited. Nashville: Thomas Nelson Co., 1991, p. 304

7) J.D. Thomas, Evolution and Faith. Abilene, TX, ACU Press, 1988. p. 81-82

8) Ali Demirsoy, Kalitim ve Evrim (Inheritance and Evolution), Ankara: Meteksan Yayinlari, 1984, p. 64

9) "Hoyle on Evolution", Nature, Vol 294, 12 November 1981, p. 105

10) Fred Hoyle, Chandra Wickramasinghe, Evolution from Space, New York, Simon & Schuster, 1984, p. 130

11) Michael Denton, Evolution: A Theory in Crisis. London: Burnett Books, 1985, p. 351

12) Pierre-P Grassé, Evolution of Living Organisms, New York: Academic Press, 1977, p. 103.

13) Pierre-P Grassé, Evolution of Living Organisms, p. 107

14) J.P. Ferris, C.T. Chen, "Photochemistry of Methane, Nitrogen, and Water Mixture As a Model for the Atmosphere of the Primitive Earth", Journal of American Chemical Society, Vol 97:11, 1975, p. 2964.

15) "New Evidence on Evolution of Early Atmosphere and Life", Bulletin of the American Meteorological Society, Vol 63, November 1982, pp. 1328-1330

16) "Life's Crucible", Earth, February 1998, p. 34

17) Colin Patterson, "Cladistics", BBC, Brian Leek ile Röportaj, Peter Franz, 4 March 1982.

18) Pierre-Paul Grassé, Evolution of Living Organisms, Academic Press, New York, 1977, p. 88

19) Charles Darwin, The Origin of Species: A Facsimile of the First Edition, Harvard University Press, 1964, p. 189

20) Derek A. Ager, "The Nature of the Fossil Record", Proceedings of the British Geological Association, Vol 87, 1976, p. 133

21) Douglas J. Futuyma, Science on Trial, New York: Pantheon Books, 1983. p. 197

22) Richard Monestarsky, "Mysteries of the Orient", Discover, April 1993, p. 40

23) Richard Dawkins, The Blind Watchmaker, London: W.W. Norton 1986, p. 229

24) Charles Darwin, The Origin of Species: A Facsimile of the First Edition, Harvard University Press, 1964, p. 302

25) David Raup, "Conflicts Between Darwin and Paleontology", Bulletin, Field Museum of Natural History, Vol 50, January 1979, p. 24

26) Gerald T. Todd, "Evolution of the Lung and the Origin of Bony Fishes: A Casual Relationship", American Zoologist, Vol 26, No. 4, 1980, p. 757

27) R.L. Carroll, Vertebrate Paleontology and Evolution, New York: W.H. Freeman and Co. 1988, p. 4.

28) Jean-Jacques Hublin, The Hamlyn Encyclopædia of Prehistoric Animals, New York: The Hamlyn Publishing Group Ltd., 1984, p. 120

29) Jacques Millot, "The Coelacanth", Scientific American, Vol 193, December 1955, p. 39

30) Bilim ve Teknik (Science and Technology), November 1998, No. 372, p. 21

31) Lewis L. Carroll, "Problems of the Origin of Reptiles" Biological Reviews of the Cambridge Philosophical Society, Vol 44. p. 393

32) Fossils of Seymouria are found in Lower Permian rocks, dated at about 280 million years. However, the earliest known reptiles Hylonomus and Paleothyris are found in Lower Pennsylvanian rocks and the Middle Pennsylvanian rocks, dated at about 310-330 million years. (See Barbara J. Stahl, Vertebrate History: Problems in Evolution, Dover, 1985, pp. 238-239)

33) Pat Shipman, "Birds do it... Did Dinosaurs?", New Scientist, 1 February 1997, p. 28

34) Nature, Vol 382, 1 August 1996, p. 401

35) L.D. Martin, J.D. Stewart, K.N. Whetstone, The Auk, Vol 98, 1980, p. 86.

36) A.H. Brush, "On the Origin of Feathers", Journal of Evolutionary Biology, Vol. 9, 1996. p. 132.

37) A.H. Brush, "On the Origin of Feathers", p. 131.

38) A.H. Brush, "On the Origin of Feathers", p. 133.

39) A.H. Brush, "On the Origin of Feathers", p. 131.

40) "Plucking the Feathered Dinosaur", Science, Vol 278, 14 November 1997, p. 1229.

41) Douglas Palmer, "Learning to Fly", (Review of The Origin of and Evolution of Birds by Alan Feduccia, Yale University Press, 1996), New Scientist, Vol 153, 1 March 1997, p. 44.

42) Norman Macbeth, Darwin Retried: An Appeal to Reason, Boston: Gambit, 1971, p. 101.

43) Roger Lewin, "Bones of Mammals, Ancestors Fleshed Out", Science, Vol 212, 26 June 1981, p. 1492.

44) George Gaylord Simpson, Life Before Man, New York: Time-Life Books, 1972, p. 42.

45) Richard E. Leakey, The Making of Mankind, Michael Joseph Limited, London 1981, p. 43

46) William R Fix,. The Bone Peddlers, Macmillan Publishing Company: New York, 1984, pp.150-153

47) Scientific American, December 1992

48) Solly Zuckerman, Beyond The Ivory Tower, New York: Toplinger Publications, 1970, pp. 75-94.

49) Charles E. Oxnard, "The Place of Australopithecines in Human Evolution: Grounds for Doubt", Nature, Vol 258, p. 389

50) Holly Smith, American Journal of Physical Anthropology, Vol 94, 1994, pp. 307-325.

51) Fred Spoor, Bernard Wood, Frans Zonneveld, "Implication of Early Hominid Labryntine Morphology for Evolution of Human Bipedal Locomotion", Nature, Vol 369, 23 June 1994, p. 645-648.

52) Boyce Rensberger, The Washington Post, 19 November 1984

53) Marvin Lubenow, Bones of Contention, Grand Rapids, Baker, 1992, p. 83

54) Richard Leakey, The Making of Mankind, London: Sphere Books, 1981, p. 62

55) Erik Trinkaus, "Hard Times Among the Neanderthals", Natural History, Vol 87, December 1978, p. 10; R.L. Holloway, "The Neanderthal Brain: What Was Primitive", American Journal of Physical Anthropology Supplement, Vol 12, 1991, p. 94

56) Alan Walker, Science, Vol 207, 1980, p. 1103.

57) A.J. Kelso, Physical Antropology, 1st ed., New York: J.B. Lipincott Co., 1970, p. 221; M.D. Leakey, Olduvai Gorge, Vol 3, Cambridge: Cambridge University Press, 1971, p. 272.

58) S.J. Gould, Natural History, Vol 85, 1976, p. 30

59) Time, 23 December 1996

60) Ruth Henke, "Aufrecht aus den Baumen", Focus, Vol 39, 1996, p. 178

61) Elaine Morgan, The Scars of Evolution, New York: Oxford University Press, 1994, p. 5

62) Earnest A. Hooton, Up From The Ape, New York: McMillan, 1931, p. 332

63) Malcolm Muggeridge, The End of Christendom, Grand Rapids, Eerdmans, 1980, p. 59.

64) Stephen Jay Gould, "Smith Woodward's Folly", New Scientist, 5 April 1979, p. 44

65) Michael Walker, Quadrant, October 1982, p.44

66) David Jorafsky, Soviet Marxism, Natural Science, p. 12

67) Malcolm Muggeridge, The End of Christendom, Grand Rapids: Eerdmans, 1980, p. 59

68) Francis Darwin, The Life and Letters of Charles Darwin, vol 1. New York, D. Appleton and Company, 1888. pp. 285-86

69) Gertrude Himmelfarb. Darwin and the Darwinian Revolution. Chatto & Windus, London, 1959. p. 348

70) Chandra Wickramasinghe, Interview in London Daily Express, August 14, 1981.

Look for other books in the series:

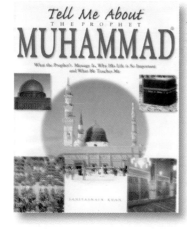

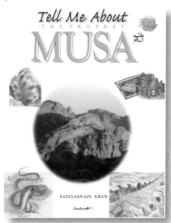

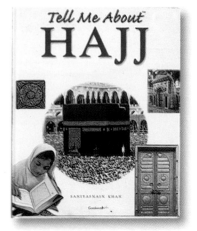